Forgiveness
Book

THE FORGIVENESS BOOK

BOB LIBBY

Authors Choice Press

New York Bloomington

The Forgiveness Book

Authors Choice Press
an imprint of iUniverse, Inc.

iUniverse books may be ordered through booksellers or by contacting:

iUniverse
1663 Liberty Drive
Bloomington, IN 47403
www.iuniverse.com
1-800-Authors (1-800-288-4677)

ISBN: 978-1-4502-4280-6 (sc)

Printed in the United States of America

iUniverse rev. date: 06/28/2010

ACKNOWLEDGMENTS

Many thanks to: Edith Cowles, Mary Marshall, Mary Weldon, Beth Baker, Ginny Habeeb, Sandy Elliott, John Ratti, Jim Simpson, Cynthia Shattuck, Leith Speiden, and the Society of St. John the Evangelist.

My gratitude to all those whose stories are shared in this book, and the Lord whose grace has unleashed the power of forgiving love in their lives.

My family and my congregations for their patience and forgiveness and love. May the Lord provide the difference between the love they needed and the love they received.

Table of Contents

Learning to Forgive: An Introduction

It was the last thing that I thought I would ever do. I had gone off to a monastery. And although I was an Episcopal priest, it wasn't an Episcopal monastery I had sought out, but a Roman Catholic one. And it wasn't just any Roman Catholic enclosure, but a Trappist establishment outside Atlanta and a place where you're not allowed to talk, or so I thought.

I had grown up in Douglaston on Long Island, near New York City. Thomas Merton had lived there for a while as a child, too. Later, he had converted from nominal Episcopalian to avid Roman Catholic and had gone off and joined a Trappist monastery in Kentucky, chronicling his spiritual journey in a bestselling book called *The Seven Storey Mountain*. The people I knew in Douglaston in general and the parishioners of Zion Episcopal Church in particular did not come off very well in Merton's book, so it was fashionable in Douglaston to be angry with Thomas Merton. In addition to that, my father, something of a refined Archie Bunker, had always been down on Roman Catholics.

So there I was in the refectory of the Monastery of the Holy Spirit in Conyers, Georgia, having lunch with Patrick, a monastery bum who stayed afloat by moving from cloister to cloister, trying to be devout and helpful in exchange for a warm bed and three meals a day. Patrick always had with him a rosary that more closely resembled a light anchor chain than a piece of personal devotional jewelry. He followed me about sharing ecclesiastical gossip, equally proficient in both Roman and Anglican monastic chatter. Patrick had made the rounds.

Father Francis, an Italian priest and the monastery's retreat master, finally rescued me by giving Patrick some chores to do. He explained Patrick's unique status: " Every monastery has them. Some say the Lord sends them to test us and try our patience. We'll let him stay around for about a week and then send him along to the next community. Before he leaves, he'll probably ask for some money. It's alright to give him a little—but don't be too generous. He's *very* persuasive."

My three days at the monastery were to constitute a pre-Lenten retreat. I came equipped to do some heavy reading, having packed both Augustine's *Confessions* and Dietrich Bonhoeffer's *The Cost of Discipleship*, along with my Bible and The Book of Common Prayer. I had really set out to impress God. But the Lord had other plans.

I quickly got into the rhythm of the community. The monks—there were about thirty of them—lived in a dormitory on the south side of the community's vast, cathedral-sized chapel. The guest house was attached to the chapel's north side, while visitors like me ate separately from the community and met the monks primarily in the chapel, starting our round of daily offices long before first light, and ending with Compline around nine in the evening. The members of the order occupied the chancel stalls. Visitors had a special section at the back of the chapel. The relatively small group of monks filled the great hall with their chants and hymns of praise.

I soon discovered that almost half of my fellow retreatants were not Roman Catholics. But Father Francis was an equal opportunity host and glided about as if on ball bearings, trying to make our stay a comfortable one. Father Francis, it turned out, was allowed to talk. So was Father Bob, the retreat master, who was available for counseling, conversation, and confession.

There was no structure to the retreat program, beyond sharing the community's daily round of offices and meals. There was a reading room and lots of space outside for walks. The brothers ran a bakery, a dairy, a fern farm, a bookstore, and a stained glass studio. Aside from the bookstore, you could watch or, in the bakery, smell the wonderful aromas, but the rule was, "Please don't talk to the monks." If you forgot yourself, they would just smile and go about their work as if you weren't there.

I couldn't seem to get interested in either Bonhoeffer or Augustine, so I browsed about in the book store for something to read. I came upon a tattered pamphlet on how to forgive as well as how to be forgiven. As I read, many old hurts given and received bubbled up. I decided that this would be a good time to seek spiritual direction and perhaps even make a confession.

For those readers who are not Episcopalians, let me explain a unique feature of our church. For Episcopalians—unlike Roman Catholics—private confession is optional. As children, we were taught in confirmation class that God would forgive us if (a) we were truly sorry for our offense and not just sorry that we got caught; (b) we intended to avoid committing the offense ever again; and (c) we intended to make amends for any wrong we had done to others. We were also taught to say our prayers daily and to ask for forgiveness. We were assured that God would indeed forgive us if all of the above conditions were met. And we were reminded to avail ourselves of the general confession in the Sunday

service. If *all else failed*, we could seek out a priest—
they all had special authority to forgive sins—and he
would be honor-bound not to tell our mothers what
we had done or what we had thought.

In seminary it was strongly recommended that,
since it was just possible some conscience-weary
parishioner might want to dump a lifetime of riotous
living in our laps, it might be a good idea to learn
what went into making and hearing a confession—
"just in case." We were also reminded that all of our
seminary faculty were priests and that they were
duty-bound not to tell our bishops anything we said
to them. Those reassurances must not have worked
for many of my classmates. I know they didn't work
for me. As a last ditch effort, the seminary faculty
devoted our entire senior retreat to the subject of
confession and forgiveness and imported an anonymous priest whom no one knew to " do the job" of
hearing our confessions.

So during that senior retreat I decided it was " now
or never." I did a careful examination of my twenty-
six years of life, and made a list of the things I had
done and the things I had not done. It was a long
list—believe me, when I looked it over again it
seemed as if indeed " there was no health in me." I remember waiting silently in line, reviewing my short
life, certain that after it was over I would be asked to
leave seminary and return to the Marine Corps, or
sell life insurance, or perhaps there was still a place
for me at the steel mill where I once worked.

When my time came, I read the list of offenses
aloud. The priest did not seem impressed. He spoke
gently of the prodigal son, of the death of Jesus on
the cross, and of Peter's reconciliation with the Lord
after the resurrection. He told me to read the
Twenty-Third Psalm and pronounced the absolution.

It was as simple as that. I was amazed and relieved as I walked away feeling like a newborn baby. In those days Billy Graham was already talking on TV about being born again, and I knew, that day, what he meant. Thereafter, making a confession became part of my spiritual discipline.

Meanwhile, back at the monastery, I began my preparation for a full confession: prayer, self-examination, making a list of the things I had done and not done, reviewing the order for the reconciliation of a penitent in The Book of Common Prayer. While I was prepared to be specific about my sins of omission and commission for the previous year, one phrase in the Prayer Book kept haunting me. After the priest has asked the penitent to elucidate his or her sins and to ask for forgiveness, these questions—and answers—occur: "Will you turn again to Christ as your Lord? I will. Do you forgive those who have sinned against you? I forgive them." It was the second phrase that kept bouncing about in my mind: "I forgive them."

I made an appointment with Father Bob, and waited in the refectory. Father Bob came at the appointed hour and led me into a small study. I had expected something else. Whatever happened to the archetypal Roman confessional made of golden oak? We sat facing each other in two overstuffed chairs.

"Aren't you going to get into a box or something?" I asked.

Father Bob smiled. "We don't do that here any more. The only box I own is a shoe box. Would it help if I turned my back?"

"No, that's alright. How do we start?"

We began with a prayer. I made my confession. He granted absolution, made a few comments, and concluded with the Lord's Prayer and a blessing. Then

Learning to Forgive: An Introduction

we sat and talked. I showed him The Book of Common Prayer and asked him about forgiving others. He thought a minute and reflected that there was as much, if not more, in the Bible about forgiving others than there was about being forgiven. We parted company with the Trappist's statement, " Let me know how you make out."

I went back to the monastery chapel and started leafing through Scripture. I then began to make a list of the people who had hurt me or let me down in some way. I prayed about each person and prayed for each, and asked God's help in forgiving them.

Some interesting things happened as I prayed. Some of the old hurts looked silly in the light of day; others seemed to have explanations, reasons that had never occurred to me. But the " hard core" situations, those that seemed to have neither explanation nor reason, were still there and it really still hurt to think of them. I prayed again to forgive and then took my list out and burned it. I had the same feeling of making a new beginning as I had after my first confession.

When we define ourselves by the people who have hurt us, or the people who hate us, we remain in bondage to those people until we are able to forgive them. When we are unable to let go of the past, our identity is defined by those moments of hatred and pain. But as Christians we are called to identify ourselves by one who loves us and was willing to die on the cross that we might have life.

I was so elated on my trip back to my parish in Orange Park, Florida, that I decided to share my experience with the small congregation that gathered for the Wednesday night service. To my surprise, their response was, " Were we on the list?" My rejoinder was, " Should you be?"

It never occurred to me at the time that my experience with the Trappists in Georgia and the subsequent spiritual fallout might make its way into a book. That's the second part of my story.

Edith Cowles was what my grandfather called, "a maiden lady school teacher." She had taught in both public and private schools and she had a large following of former students going back some thirty years. Miss Edith could make the English language come alive; she loved the sound of words, the cadence of a well-crafted sentence, and the rhythm of poetry. In college she was known as the Edna St. Vincent Millay of the school. She wrote and published her poetry, edited a book of short essays by Harriet Beecher Stowe, and presided over the literary society.

Miss Edith became my mentor and my friend; when I had a writing project, I would pay her a visit and ask her advice. She was always gentle with me, and she never said, "When are you ever going to learn how to spell?" She was more likely to ask, "Do you spell reconciliation with one or two L's?"

As short stories about people, places, and happenings began to pile up, we often talked about doing a book, but nothing happened until years later when Miss Edith was dying of cancer.

"Whatever happened to our book?" she asked after we had shared Holy Communion one afternoon.

I told her that I had lost interest and that most of the material was hopelessly dated.

"True, true," she replied, "but some of it isn't. There are a number of stories that will never be out of date. They're about forgiveness."

Learning to Forgive: An Introduction

Edith and I had been talking a lot about forgiveness. She was, in her words, "cramming for my finals." She had made her own list of people who had hurt her or let her down, and was struggling to forgive and let go of old pain.

"Why don't you start with the few you've got and build on them? Write stories about forgiveness. You could call it *The Forgiveness Book*."

And so I have.

On the following pages, you will find a collection of short stories. Some were in the original collection, and the rest have been added since my conversation with Miss Edith. Each one stands by itself, but the common thread is forgiveness—asking for it, receiving it, forgiving oneself, forgiving others, and being reconciled. In most of the stories more than one element of forgiveness is present, although one may dominate.

Following each story, I have included a brief Bible passage, some thoughts for reflection, and a prayer. The twenty-two chapters are followed by an afterword, which tries to relate my sketches to the work of Christ on the cross. Finally, at the back of the book, you will find further biblical resources and various forms for self-examination. The book is intended as a "first reader" in forgiveness, and most of the stories deal with the personal aspects of forgiveness. There are other, corporate dimensions to forgiveness, particularly the link between forgiveness and justice, but this is a *first* reader. You can use it for private reading and devotions, or in groups for Adult Christian Education or Lenten study programs.

Read the stories in any order you like. Skip around if that's your style. Each story stands on its own. All are true, although in many cases names have been changed for obvious reasons. This isn't my book any-

more. You bought it. You paid for it. It's your forgiveness book.

Working the Graveyard Shift

Back in my college years, I had a job in a steel foundry, working the graveyard shift. The E.V. Camp Steel Works was located in what were then the outskirts of Atlanta, near Decatur, Georgia. The foundry straddled a siding of the Seaboard Coast Line Railroad.

Camp was known in the steel industry as a marginal producer. During World War II the foundry had been in full production, but in the shift to a peace time economy, it had closed down. The Korean War revived the need for steel and Camp reopened part of its facilities. Freight trains delivered gondola cars loaded with rusting scrap steel to the siding and we would recycle it. Our main bread-and-butter items were 3,500-pound steel ingots which were shipped on to the rolling mills of Caterpillar Tractor in Peoria, Illinois. The money makers were specialty items made from armor plate steel.

I was a pre-theological student at Emory University when, in the summer of 1951, I began working at E.V.Camp as a laborer. However, when the people at Camp discovered that I had basic college credits in chemistry, I was offered a job in the company laboratory on the 11 p.m.—7 a.m. shift. My task was to run all the analyses on each heat of steel that was poured, which included making a preliminary test about ten minutes before they were finished "cooking up a batch." I would approach the mouth of the furnace with a long "spoon." The foreman would, ever so gently, pour a cup of molten steel into my "spoon" and I would rush into my lab to find out whether, among other things, it needed more or less carbon. If more carbon was required, powdered charcoal was added to the mixture. If less was needed, a ceramic hose was inserted, which bubbled oxygen through the liquid steel. The fiery, bubbling mixture was always a spectacle to behold, especially at night, with sparks flying in all directions.

When I look back on that last year of college, I wonder how I ever kept the pace I set for myself. The graveyard shift at Camp was followed by a drive back to the dorm to shower and shave, have breakfast on the run, go to classes from 8:30-12:30, sleep in the afternoon, have dinner at 7:00, hit the library until 10:15, and then head out North Druid Hills Road to the steel plant to start the next graveyard shift.

In about a month, I had the lab routine under control and there was time to study and even nod off a bit between periods of peak performance, but somehow I could never manage to stay fully awake between 4 and 5 a.m. At that point in the shift, I always got a sinking feeling and had to put my head down on a laboratory table, if only for a few minutes.

One of my minor duties, by the way, was to be in charge of the first aid kit. Hardly an evening went by that I didn't apply a dab of burn ointment or a band-aid or two to an injured worker. The case I remember most vividly was the one that began when Joshua and Jeremiah Bentley appeared in the lab about 4 a.m. Josh and Jerry were twins. They owned small farms in nearby Gwinnett County. They farmed by day and came to the foundry at night, where they always worked as a team.

I was awakened from one of my quick naps by the twins. They were quiet men and apologized for dis-

Working the Graveyard Shift

turbing me. Josh was obviously in pain. Jerry explained that he—Jerry—had dropped a small
(hundred pound) ingot on his brother's foot. "I didn't
mean to do it, Josh; I really didn't mean to do it," he
kept assuring his twin. "It's OK, Jerry...it's okay...I
know you didn't mean to do it. I forgive you."

It was a company regulation that all of us wear
steel-capped safety shoes. Unfortunately, at the time
of the accident Josh had been wearing his regular
farm boots. It quickly became obvious that the boot
could not be removed and that some real damage
had been done to the foot, so I checked out with the
foreman and drove Josh and Jerry to the emergency
room at Emory University Hospital. All the way there,
Jerry kept telling his brother, "I didn't mean to do it,
Josh. I didn't mean to do it."

The resident on duty at the hospital had to cut
Josh's boot off. Several bones were broken. Jerry
looked on as the foot was put in a cast. "I didn't
mean to hurt you. I didn't mean to do it!" was Jerry's
constant litany as we drove back to the plant in the
first light of the new day.

It was several weeks later that Jerry hobbled into
my office. It was obvious that he had hurt his foot. I
could see that the scenario of the previous month
had been repeated in almost every detail; the only
variation was that Jerry had dropped the steel ingot
on his *own* foot.

As I drove Jerry back from the emergency room, he
actually seemed happy as he reassured me once
more, "I didn't mean to hurt Josh." In his own
strange way, Jerry had evened the score.

For Reflection
*But he was wounded for our transgressions,
crushed for our iniquities; upon him was the punish-*

*ment that made us whole, and by his bruises we are
healed* (Is. 53:5).

One of the most mysterious and poignant passages in the Bible is the prophet Isaiah's description
of the Suffering Servant. It expresses the idea of one
who would voluntarily accept the punishment that
was deserved by another: " He was wounded for our
transgressions."

The passage echoes the central idea of the Jewish
Day of Atonement. According to the Book of Leviti-
cus, the priest was to choose two goats, one for a
sacrifice and one for the *azazel*. The ritual of the
azazel, or scapegoat, had its roots deep within the
nomadic culture. Each year an animal was chosen to
carry the sins and hostilities of the community off
into the wilderness. The poor creature would be
yelled at, beaten, spit upon, and driven out of town
to die, taking the spiritual garbage of the community
with him.

Christians like St. Paul were quick to see a reflection of this figure in Jesus, " whom God put forward
as an expiation by his blood, to be received through
faith" (Rom. 3:25). So it is that we see in Jesus the
one who has taken away our sins.

What a simple idea it is, and yet how difficult it is
for us to believe it...and so we go on punishing ourselves as Jerry did on the graveyard shift.

Why is it that we have such trouble accepting forgiveness from others? Why is it we have trouble for
giving ourselves?

Teach us to forgive ourselves for all these sins, O
forgiving God, and help us to overcome them.
*For all these sins, O God of mercy, forgive us, par-
don us, grant us atonement!* —Liturgy for the Day of
Atonement, Reform Tradition

Working the Graveyard Shift

The Prodigal Father

It was a strange kind of encounter. I had never been a photographer's model before, but there I was posing—or, more correctly, waiting to pose—as Ron Smithfield set up his equipment in old St. Margaret's Church. When I had agreed to pose, I had no idea it would be so complicated or that it would take more than fifteen or twenty minutes at the most. But we had been in the church for over an hour and Ron had yet to take one exposure.

Ron was an airline pilot by trade and a photographer by choice. His airline duties took up only sixty hours a month—for which he earned a six-digit salary. That left plenty of time and money to pursue his art. Ron's home, which was within walking distance of the church, was a veritable gallery of his photographs: shots of sunlight filtering through Spanish moss, old pilings defining a broken course in the St. John's River, water hyacinths engulfing an old orange crate.

The project at hand was to be part of his "old country church" portfolio. St. Margaret's was a classic example of American Carpenter Gothic. Built in 1875, it had begun life as a plantation chapel. The original parishioners and many of their descendants had been buried in straggly rows in the cemetery that took up much of the churchyard. Furthermore, Eugenia Price had set one of her historical novels here and a CBS film crew made a generous donation to the church restoration fund in exchange for the right to do a "made-for-TV" movie. Azalea bushes, ancient live oak trees, and a weathered picket fence completed the scene.

As Ron explained his project, it struck me that I was to be the "old country parson" to go with his "old country church." My job was to stand fully vested at the altar, pulpit, or lectern, and look either prayerful or concerned. My white robe and white hair would be contrasted with the dark wood paneling, the stained glass, and the flickering candles. Almost an hour had passed, and Ron still was not satisfied with the lighting. At that point our conversation, which had been on the light side, became more serious.

"Is your father still living?" Ron asked me.

"No," I answered, "he died about eight years ago."

"Did you see your father often?"

"Once or twice a year."

"Were you like your father?"

"We didn't look much like each other. My sisters looked like Dad. I took after my mother's side of the family. They said I looked a lot like my grandfather. What about you, Ron?" I asked.

Ron got down off a stepladder and leaned against a pew.

"I never knew my father until about a month ago," he said.

He told me that his mother and father had divorced when he was a baby. His mother had moved back to the East Coast and started a new life. All Ron knew about his father was that he came from Kansas City and that, in his mother's opinion, he was "not a nice person."

"What happened a month ago?"

Ron's flight assignment had been switched and he had found himself with a twenty-four-hour layover in Kansas City.

The Prodigal Father

"Curiosity got the better of me and I picked up the phone book to see if by any chance my father's name was in the book. And there it was, Ronald M. Smithfield. I started to dial the number five or six times before I had the courage to let the call ring through."

"The conversation was awkward at first," Ron continued. "But there was no doubt the man in the phone book was my dad. At first he gave me very little information about himself or his circumstances, and he was reluctant to agree to a meeting. Finally, he said that he would run by my hotel at 7:30 a.m. for a quick cup of coffee on his way to work."

"I agreed to wear my pilot's uniform and he, in turn, would be wearing a blue alligator sports shirt. In case that wasn't enough, I would have him paged at 7:40 am."

It turned out that none of the signals and precautions was necessary. Ron spotted his father the minute he came through the door of the hotel lobby.

"I thought I was looking in a mirror, except that his hair was steel gray. If you had put us side by side, we would have looked like the 'before' and 'after' in a Grecian Formula ad."

Their thirty-minute cup of coffee lasted well into the afternoon. It turned out that Ron's father was a professional photographer and an amateur pilot.

"We had so much in common," Ron said, "that it was like finding a piece of myself."

Ron bubbled over with an avalanche of details and, as he finally snapped his first picture of me, he asked, "I wonder if meeting God will be like that?"

For Reflection

Philip said to him, "Lord, show us the Father, and we will be satisfied." Jesus said to him, "Have I been with you all this time, Philip, and you still do not know me? Whoever has seen me has seen the Father" (Jn. 14:8-9).

One of the best definitions I have ever heard of the word "sin" is that it is separation—separation from God, separation from others, and separation from oneself. I cannot think of any sin that does not separate us from one or all of the above.

The consequence of Ron's parents' divorce was that he was separated, not only from his natural father, but, as he was to discover, from a significant part of himself. Ron not only didn't know who and what his father was, but what information he did have was bad information.

As I have reflected on this story, I have come to see it more and more as a parable of our relationship to God. The scriptural account of the Garden of Eden tells of a time when God and human beings were very close to each other. God came and walked with Adam and Eve in the garden in the cool of the evening. Then came what C.S. Lewis has called "the great divorce": we were separated from God and became "strangers and aliens." Not only did we not know God, but what information we did have was erroneous or distorted. The work of Jesus as expressed in the passage above was not only meant to tell us about the Father, but to show us what God the Father is like. "Whoever has seen me has seen the Father."

You might want to ask yourself whether or not your own relationship to God is clouded with misinformation. When you think of the issues involving forgiveness, is your thinking distorted by a picture of God as an angry old man, or as someone who "doesn't give a damn"? Do we have so much bad information that we are afraid to get close—or are we just not interested?

The Prodigal Father

Jesus spoke to us about God who was his Father and who is " our Father." He even used the Aramaic word *Abba* when speaking of God; *Abba* is the equivalent of "Daddy." You might want to reflect on how an understanding of God as *Abba* might change your life.

Most loving Father, whose will it is for us to give thanks for all things, to fear nothing but the loss of you, and to cast all our care on you who care for us: Preserve us from faithless fears and worldly anxieties, that no clouds of this mortal life may hide from us the light of that love which is immortal, and which you have manifested to us in your Son Jesus Christ our Lord; who lives and reigns with you, in the unity of the Holy Spirit, one God, now and for ever. —The Book of Common Prayer

Passing the Peace

Passing the peace, when it was first introduced to the Episcopal Church, seemed to some people more like a declaration of war. Scholars had rediscovered the practice in ancient books of worship from the early church. The basic idea was that worshippers would greet each other in the Lord. You would either extend your right hand to those around you or embrace your nearest and dearest Christian neighbors. Some thought this looked mighty like a good old Baptist "Greet your neighbor," or maybe acting out the AT&T slogan, "Reach out and touch someone," or even the seventh inning stretch at Yankee Stadium.

But we were assured by scholars that the peace was an ancient and apostolic practice that "completed the penitential order of the service." By this, they meant that it followed the general confession and the absolution—the pronouncement of God's forgiveness of our sins. Furthermore, it was in keeping with the biblical injunction found in the Gospel of Matthew, "First be reconciled to your brother or sister, and then come and offer your gift."

"You don't expect me to shake hands with someone I haven't even spoken to in years, do you?" was a typical comment that only underscored the need for just such a liturgical activity.

Some complained that the peace was a carry-over from one of those "touchy-feely encounter groups that meet in hot tubs." One venerable priest—devoted to the old way of doing most everything—would drop to his knees when he saw it coming and busy himself by filing his complaints with the Almighty until the peace had indeed passed him by.

Oh, there were some who took to the idea, behaving as if the passing of the peace signaled the beginning of a "get acquainted" hour; these people would run around the church like little boys in dancing school, seeing how many names they could get on their dance cards. Others dealt with the peace as if it were a military maneuver. I remember seeing one such approach while attending an early morning eucharist in the Bethlehem Chapel at the National Cathedral in Washington. When it came time to exchange the peace, an older gentleman marched about with the precision of a wind-up toy soldier, extending his hand to other worshippers and just as quickly withdrawing it. The old martinet didn't miss a soul in the congregation. In fact, he also greeted two stone columns without blinking an eye!

All this is by way of background for an incident that brought home to me the penitential nature of the peace.

I was at the General Convention of the Episcopal Church in Denver, Colorado, in 1979. The Florida delegation gathered each day at the end of the legislative session to "caucus." It was better known as the "happy hour." We were more than halfway through the grueling, two-week session, and weariness was beginning to set in.

Then it happened. I got into a fight with Gerald, a fellow priest whom I had known since seminary. You understand, it wasn't a fist fight, but a good sharp verbal encounter. We squared off and exchanged sarcasms to the horror of the delegation—not to mention the bishop and both our wives. It was all over in sixty seconds, in time to go out to an Italian restaurant for dinner, where Gerald and I kept our distance for the evening. We apologized publicly in the morning, but things between us just weren't the same.

Three months later, at a diocesan gathering, I was standing in the back of the cathedral. The bishop declared, " The peace of the Lord be always with you."

" And also with you," we replied.

I turned to the right, left, and then the rear—and there stood Gerald. He was as uncomfortable about the whole transaction as I was.

The same thing happened two months later. This time, however, when we faced each other for the third time, it finally happened. We broke into laughter and almost into tears. Then we threw our arms around each other.

" The peace of the Lord be with you, Gerald."

" And also with you, Bob."

For Reflection

You have heard that it was said to those of ancient times, "You shall not murder"; and "whoever murders shall be liable to judgment." But I say to you that if you are angry with a brother or sister, you will be liable to judgment; and if you insult a brother or sister, you will be liable to the council; and if you say, "You fool," you will be liable to the hell of fire. So when you are offering your gift at the altar, if you remember that your brother or sister has something against you, leave your gift there before the altar and go; first be reconciled to your brother or sister, and then come and offer your gift (Mt. 5:21-24).

I asked a detective at the local sheriff's office what he thought was the chief cause of murder. " Anger and resentment," was his instant response. He went on to say that 85% of all murders occur within family or friendship groups: 85% of murder victims are known by their murderers, and only 15% of murder victims are killed by strangers.

This is certainly true in the biblical account of the first murder where, in Genesis 4, Cain slew his brother Abel.

In the biblical scheme of things, crime and sin begin in the heart and mind before they are acted out in murder, adultery, perjury, or theft. This idea is certainly reinforced by Jesus in the Sermon on the Mount. Before murder comes slander, and before that, name calling, and before that, resentment and bad feelings. Our Lord's suggestion is to deal with broken relationships immediately.

To paraphrase Matthew 5:21-24, "Don't dehumanize others so that you can justify being angry with them. And if you are in church and remember that you and your brother, sister, friend, spouse, neighbor, business partner, teammate are out of relationship, stop right there! Don't even wait for the collection plate to be passed. Leave the church and go make up with them. Then come back to church."

Forgiveness and reconciliation were top priority items for Jesus and the church of the New Testament. They should be top priorities for us, too. If you want to make a serious examination of your relationships, turn to the back of this book, where you will find a form for this purpose.

Almighty and everlasting God, who in the Paschal mystery established the new covenant of reconciliation: Grant that all who have been reborn into the fellowship of Christ's Body may show forth in their lives what they profess by their faith; through Jesus Christ our Lord, who lives and reigns with you and the Holy Spirit, one God, for ever and ever. —The Book of Common Prayer

"It Doesn't Do No Good To Hate"

Willie Chappelle was black. And he was a big man and bald. Except for his dark skin, he looked like Yul Brynner. It was early in 1967 that Willie and I first met. I was in the process of resigning the rectorship of St. Catherine's, Jacksonville, to take up another job in New York, and he had been hired by the vestry to be the custodian of the church. He was not a young man and so the parishioners were somewhat surprised to see him shadowed by twin boys of pre-school age. The boys would help him empty trash cans and then run off to play on the field behind the church. When they appeared on weekday mornings as well as Saturday, the logical next step was to invite them to join the parish day school kindergarten, which ran from nine to twelve. Willie was free to do his work, the twins were in class, the school was integrated, and, surprisingly, everybody was happy.

One question remained: Where was Mrs. Chappelle? "Dead" was the answer we got. The details were a long time coming.

Three years earlier there had been a great deal of racial unrest in Jacksonville. It's difficult now to remember how bad things were then. On one especially tense day, Sears sold out of axe handles in thirty minutes. The mayor deputized the fire department on TV.

Mrs. Chappelle was walking home along Edgewood Avenue in the northwest part of town. She had been to the grocery store and was carrying a brown sack in her arms. It was time to prepare supper for the family—including her one-year-old twins.

A car came down the road. Armed with beer cans, the attackers hung out of the car windows. A shot rang out. Mrs. Chappelle's body rolled into the ditch. The car raced on. Beer cans rattled on the road. Other shots were heard. Road signs were punctured.

Willie told me the story. Then I remembered having read it in the newspaper. It had not been on the front page—there was too much going on downtown. Besides, in those days, Southern papers still had a long way to go before the murder of a black woman would make the headlines.

I was so struck by Willie's calm as he related the story of his wife's murder that I told him how impressed I was with his ability to relive the painful events without the anger I was feeling, just listening to him.

"For a year I hurt so bad and I hated so much that I couldn't look at a white man without wanting to kill him," Willie said. "Then, one night, I was putting the boys to bed and I was saying their 'Now I lay me down to sleep' with them when the Lord told me, 'Willie, it don't do no good to hate.'"

"These boys need a lot of love. You can't give 'em love when you're hating all the time. You've got to love."

For Reflection

Love is patient; love is kind; love is not envious or boastful or arrogant or rude. It does not insist on its own way; it is not irritable or resentful; it does not rejoice in wrongdoing, but rejoices in the truth (1 Cor. 13:4-6).

In the course of my priesthood, I have ministered to the families of at least six murder victims. For each of them, in different ways, the event was tragic. When the murderer is not apprehended, when justice is not done, it is doubly difficult for the family to work through their grief. A crime that is the product of racism not only is an abomination to the whole community, but leaves the family involved with additional scars so deep that it takes a miracle to heal the wounds.

To be a parent under normal circumstances takes a special measure of grace. Double that for being a single parent. What would it take to raise twin boys whose mother had been gunned down in the backlash of a race riot? Willie Chappelle knew that his boys would need a lot of love...love that is patient and kind...not irritable or resentful. Some translations read, "keeps no record of wrongs." Willie certainly had a perfect right to keep a record of the wrongs that had been done to his wife, the mother of his boys. But he knew that somehow he had to let them go so he could give his sons the love they needed.

We need to pray for an end to racism and for an end to violence that is racially motivated. We also need to pray for the victims of crime, especially for the victims of crimes where justice has not been done.

Think also about the old wounds and resentments that are blocking the flow of love in your own life. What would it take to let go of the "record of wrongs" that you are carrying with you?

O Lord, you have taught us that without love whatever we do is worth nothing, Send your Holy Spirit and pour into our hearts your greatest gift, which is love, the true bond of peace and of all virtue, without which whoever lives is accounted dead before you. Grant this for the sake of your only Son Jesus Christ, who lives and reigns with you and the Holy Spirit, one God, now and forever. —The Book of Common Prayer

Easter Eggs for the Bishop

O n a summer evening in 1990, Emilio Hernandez, Episcopal Bishop of Cuba since 1980, sat with me on the balcony of a borrowed apartment on Key Biscayne. We could see the lights of Miami's skyline in the distance. Down the street, we could make out the location of the old Nixon presidential compound, most recently occupied by a now-incarcerated pal of Manuel Noriega. Down the hall was the apartment of the great-great-grandniece of Napoleon Bonaparte. An interesting assortment of historical footnotes for one quiet evening.

Bishop Hernandez was on sabbatical. It was a good time for him to be out of Cuba. The embassies in Havana were filling up with dissidents seeking asylum, while the bookies on Calle Ocho were making wagers on how long it would be before Cuba went the way of Poland, East Germany, and Czechoslovakia.

While Bishop Hernandez and I talked on the balcony, his wife Edivia sat inside watching Miami's Channel 23, an independent Spanish-language television station.

Anyone living in or around Miami soon discovers that time in the Cuban community is measured B.C. and A.C.—Before Castro and After Castro—and Hernandez was no exception. B.C., in 1955, he had been ordained a priest of the Iglesia Episcopal de Cuba, identified himself with the revolutionary forces, and joined the 26 July Movement called, in Spanish, *Cuba Civicia Democratica*. Hernandez described himself as a young revolutionary, deeply offended by the brutality, injustice, and exploitation of Cuba's right-wing Batista dictatorship. The future bishop of Cuba had cheered Castro's triumph in 1959, and for a short time after that worked in Florencia, coordinating the construction and development of new schools.

"Castro said that he was not a communist," Hernandez told me. "But his people began to make jokes about it and ridicule those who raised questions about some of his Marxist statements." When, in 1961, Castro declared himself to be a communist, Hernandez disassociated himself from Castro. "I was disappointed, disillusioned...so I dropped out."

Castro took 45,000 political prisoners. Most of them were former revolutionaries, former followers of his own movement.

On July 19, 1962, while serving at the Church of San Lucas in Santiago de Cuba, Hernandez was arrested and jailed, first locally, but eventually in the prison on Isla de Pinos, made infamous in Armando Valladares' memoir, *Against All Hope.*

Hernandez served his full ten-year sentence, declining to shorten his stay by attending "political rehabilitation" classes. During his time in prison, visits from his family were infrequent and highly restricted. Reading material was forbidden; the most popular food items allowed were hard-boiled eggs. His wife Edivia happened to notice that the prison guards, while closely inspecting the eggs, ignored the papers in which she wrapped them. From that day forward, deliveries of hard-boiled eggs were wrapped in pages of Scripture and the Book of Common Prayer. That way Hernandez's personal devotions were enriched—as well as his diet.

I am certain that his prison experience had a lot to do with a statement Bishop Hernandez made to my congregation in Orange Park, Florida, in 1988: " By the grace of God, when I left prison on July 21, 1972, I was able to walk out a free man...free not only physically, but free spiritually."

Sitting on the balcony in Key Biscayne, he reflected on his hardwon spiritual freedom.

" During all my lifetime, I have learned that forgiveness is the best spiritual cure for the mind and the body....When I was a young man, I fought against injustice. I even fought with my hands. But when I saw all that anger come out of me, I felt ashamed. I was sorry, and many times I asked for and experienced forgiveness.

" When I came out of prison, I prayed that I might be able to forgive. My prayer was answered. I came out a free spirit. Many of my friends came out bitter and hateful. They were traumatized. Some never recovered.

" I thank God that I am a free man."

For Reflection

For freedom Christ has set us free. Stand firm, therefore, and do not submit again to a yoke of slavery (Gal. 5.1).

The theme of freedom and liberation is a recurring one in both the Hebrew Bible and Christian Scriptures. Liberation from slavery and oppression in Egypt, signified by the Passover event, is at the very heart of the Jewish experience. But as any student of the Bible knows, crossing the Red Sea was the easy part. After that, the children of Israel had to learn to live as free men and women under God's dominion.

Similarly, in the New Testament, the work of Christ is seen as the major liberating event of all history. In his *Religions of Man*, Houston Smith notes that the unique thing about the early Christians was their liberation from sin, self, and death. But it was still necessary for St. Paul in his Letter to the Galatians to caution the liberated Christians not to submit again to " a yoke of slavery."

Certainly hatred, resentment, and bitterness are a direct route back to bondage, as well as excess baggage that we do not have to carry. You might want to ask yourself if you are not bearing some burdens that would be better left at the foot of the cross if you are to enjoy the freedom of Christ.

O God, the Father of all, whose Son commanded us to love our enemies: Lead them and us from prejudice to truth; deliver them and us from hatred, cruelty, and revenge; and in your good time enable us all to stand reconciled before you; through Jesus Christ our Lord. —The Book of Common Prayer

Suffer the Little Children

The program did not call for singing the Navy Hymn at the end of the communion service, but somehow it seemed appropriate on that Sunday in late August at the Church of the Good Samaritan.

As the last communicant left the altar rail, Patrick and Sarah Daniel reappeared and knelt with their children. Patrick, a Navy pilot, was being deployed for six months of overseas duty. The Daniels had requested special prayers for Patrick's safe return and for the family's protection while he was gone. As the congregation sang, " Oh, hear us when we call to thee for those who serve in air and sea," I placed my hands in blessing on the couple's heads and then on Lillian, age thirteen, Elizabeth, nine, and Martha, three. Martha, with one arm bandaged from shoulder to wrist, looked up and whispered, "Thank you, Father Bob."

Martha was not the Daniels' natural child, but a " medically dependent foster care child" who had been with the family for almost a year. Sarah, a nurse, with the support of Patrick, Lill, and Beth, had worked a miracle. Martha's smiling face was a sharp contrast to the ugly, screaming, battered child I had first met a few months ago.

The bandages, which now covered only her right arm and shoulder, had once shrouded her entire body. When Martha was less than two years old, she had been raped by her uncle, an adolescent in his mid-teens. When she resisted, he forced her into the bathtub and turned on the scalding hot water.

When Martha first came to Patrick and Sarah's house, there were raw wounds on the top of her head, down her back, across her hips, and over her legs. Her right arm had been so badly scalded that the doctors were seriously considering amputation. Responsibility for Martha involved a daily routine of bathing and redressing the wounds, numerous flights to the Shriners Burn Hospital in Galveston, and dealing with a cantankerous child in constant pain who had learned how to manipulate everyone around her with her screams and cries.

A tough and disciplined love was in order. The tender cuddling, rocking, and kissing from Patrick, Sarah, and their two daughters were moderated when Martha went into a tantrum. "On occasion," said Sarah, "we even used the laying on of hands with prayer on the one unscalded cheek of her buttocks. I mean that seriously, in the full Christian sense of what the laying on of hands means. It was a form of loving discipline that conveyed power and authority for healing."

I dropped in on the Daniels one afternoon. Sarah was in the bathroom with Martha going through their daily routine of bathing the raw wounds and removing the dead scabs so that healthy skin could grow.

"We're in the bathroom," yelled Sarah. "Come on in." I started down the hall and hesitated for a moment. How would Martha respond to the presence of a male in a setting similar to that of the original assault?

"Come on in, Father Bob," squealed Martha's tiny voice. I sat on the commode and watched in amazement. Sarah had turned the painful procedure into a game in which Martha could be the leader, not the victim. Sarah would pour warm water over the child's left arm and Martha would find a scab in need of removal. Sarah would praise her for her discovery and the two would apply the tweezers and pull together. Little tears were assuaged with a kiss and praise for being so brave.

"We had to teach Martha what love was all about from the ground up. She had nothing to go on. First we tried to demonstrate what loves means and let her know that she was loved."

A daily litany began, "God loves Martha, Jesus loves Martha." Mama (Sarah), Papa (Patrick), Lillian, Elizabeth, assorted dogs and cats, and even Father Bob were on the list. Then Sarah and Patrick would pose the question, "Who loves Martha?"

"God loves Martha. Jesus loves Martha"...on down the list.

One day, Martha asked, "Does Norman love me?" Norman was her uncle, the boy who had scalded her in the bathtub.

"Oh God, what shall I say?" thought Sarah. A quick prayer, a deep gulp, and she stated, "When you love someone, you don't hurt them. Norman burned you and he's a bad boy."

"Oh," said Martha, and busied herself with her doll's dress.

There was some talk of forgiveness and prayers for Norman, but Martha wasn't through with the issue.

Then Patrick and Sarah began to ask, "Who does Martha love?"

"Martha loves God, Jesus, Mama, Papa, Lillian, Beth, Father Bob, Papa Joe..."

One day she added, "Martha loves Norman."

"Do you remember when Norman hurt you in the bath and you cried?"

"I remember," she winced.

Suffer the Little Children

"Martha, it's okay to be mad at Norman if you want to be," said Sarah, not wanting the pain to be buried deep in Martha, where it might fester and re-emerge years later.

"Where is he?" Martha asked.

"Norman is in the hospital."

"Why is he in the hospital?"

"Because he's sick."

"Sick?"

"His head is sick. That's why he did those terrible things."

"I don't want to be mad at Norman. I love him."

They prayed for Norman and for his healing.

"From that point on," said Sarah, "we saw a change in her behavior. Some inner healing had taken place. Before, Martha would avoid young men in stores and the male teens at church. All of a sudden that changed. She would let the number one acolyte at church pick her up and carry her about. Something had happened inside."

Martha's residence with the Daniels was not permanent. Eventually she went back to her natural parents, a couple barely into their twenties. The Daniels' final task was to reacquaint parents and child, and prepare them for the job of parenting.

The first visit was a disaster. Martha's mother and father arrived looking terrified and on the defensive; Martha immediately sensed their vulnerability and reverted to all of her old terror tactics. Patrick, over the cries of Martha and the protests of her natural parents, made a decision to take charge, so Martha was firmly but gently placed kicking and screaming in her crib.

Teaching these two how to be parents also had some unexpected dimensions. Sarah remembers coming home one night from an officers' wives' meeting to find Patrick shaking his head and smiling. Martha's parents had been by for a visit. Patrick said, " I take this role-modeling seriously, but never in my imagination did I ever think that I would spend an evening showing Martha's parents how to use dental floss. I sent them home with a lifetime supply!"

For Reflection

You have heard that it was said, "You shall love your neighbor and hate your enemy." But I say to you, Love your enemies and pray for those who persecute you, so that you may be children of your Father in heaven (Mt. 5:43-45).

There are many paradoxes in the teachings of Jesus: law and grace, justice and mercy. In the case of child abuse, think of Jesus' declaration that those who would harm a little child should have a millstone fastened around their neck and be thrown into the sea. But Jesus also commands us to forgive...even our enemies.

We do not need to be reminded that child abuse is evil or that we should do everything in our power to prevent it. The question before us is, rather, how to free the victim from the emotional and spiritual crippling that almost always follows. In the story of Martha, there is no doubt that her body will bear the scars of her assault, yet there is also the strong possibility that her spirit has been liberated from the emotional scars of her abuse.

You might want to reflect on how the ministry of the Daniel family helped to heal Martha's wounds. What role did tough love play? What effect did prayer have on Martha? On those who were caring for her? How was Martha's identity being changed by the care she was receiving from her foster family?

One of the recurring themes of this book is that when we are unable to let go of the past and so to forgive, our identity is defined by who we hate and who has hurt us. Through our baptismal covenant, our identity is defined by Jesus, who loves us and who died on the cross that we might have life. How does this apply to Martha's life? How does it apply to your life?

Turn the hearts of the parents to the children, and the hearts of the children to the parents; and so enkindle fervent charity among us all, that we may evermore be kindly affectioned one to another; through Jesus Christ our Lord. —The Book of Common Prayer

His First Haircut

His name was Laddie Kadoo. That really was his name—I wouldn't dare make it up. When we first met, he was three and a half and I was five. I had just moved with my family to Bay Avenue and I set out on my scooter to explore the neighborhood, or at least as much of the neighborhood as I could view from the *south* side of Bay Avenue. I wasn't allowed to cross the street without an adult or at least without holding the hand of one of my big sisters.

Laddie lived three doors down from us in a Victorian house that was painted yellow and had a fence around it with a big yellow gate that matched the house. We met at the gate and held as much of a conversation as two young lads of our years could muster. One point was perfectly clear: Laddie was not allowed out of his yard and no one was allowed in without his mother's permission.

Two days later, Laddie Kadoo's gate swung open and I was invited in. His backyard was fully equipped with swings, slide, and sand box. He also had a playroom in the basement of the house with a stash of toys: tractors, cars, trains, building blocks, and Lincoln Logs. We became fast friends.

It was a year later that Laddie had his first haircut. By now, he was allowed to go out of his yard if his mother knew where he was going, and if he promised not to cross the street. We were playing in my yard that day and found a pair of rusty old scissors. We amused ourselves by trying to cut the grass with them, by slicing up leaves, and by creating patterns in old scraps of cardboard. I don't know who brought up the subject of haircuts first, but Laddie did say that his mother was planning to take him down to the barber shop near the train station for a haircut. He had long, curly blond hair that almost touched his shoulders.

One thing led to another. It seemed foolish, we decided, to bother taking the trip to the barber shop when I had considerable experience with haircutting. I remember trying to emulate the barber by grabbing fistfuls of his hair with my left hand while chopping off curls with the scissors held in my right.

But somehow I couldn't seem to get the desired effect. I did find a comb but that didn't seem to help much. Then I remembered that the barber often wet my hair before giving it the finishing touches. So Laddie and I went over to the birdbath—which was conveniently full. I doused his head thoroughly, combed his hair out, and started cutting again.

I wasn't totally satisfied with my efforts, but Laddie seemed pleased with the work I had done and headed right home to show his mother.

The phone was ringing as I walked up the stairs in our house and headed for my room. Mother soon appeared at the door. "What did you do to Laddie Kadoo's hair?" she demanded.

"I cut it."

"You what?" Mother was very upset. Mrs. Kadoo, she reported, was in tears. Mr. Kadoo, Mother had learned, was consulting their lawyer—maybe even calling the police.

I tried my best to explain. Little by little it dawned on me that I was in real trouble. I led Mother to the scene of the crime and she picked up what scraps of hair she could find and put them in a cigar box. I was sent to my room—"until your father comes home."

The next morning, I learned, Laddie had a private, emergency appointment at the barber's. Radical remedial surgery was required. Laddie came home looking like the convicted Nazi collaborators in France at the end of World War Two.

There were no lawsuits or police at the door, although I spent one sleepless night waiting to be hauled off and thrown into a dungeon. I lost my allowance to pay for Laddie's "real" haircut. But the most severe penalty was that Laddie and I were no longer allowed to play together and, of course, I was not allowed through the yellow gate and into their yard. Like Adam of old, I was expelled from the garden.

The sentence held for six months while Laddie's hair grew back in. And, it seemed to me, it was growing back much darker—although I could only observe from a safe distance. I would ride my bike down Bay Avenue and Laddie would come to the gate and wave. If I stopped to talk, Mrs. Kadoo would come out on the porch and shoo me away. It was not easy being a pariah at six.

I finally decided to write a letter to Laddie's mother. I had started learning to write at school and I got some help from one of my sisters. "Dear Misskadoo," I wrote, "I sorry I cut Ladys hair. I thought I do him a favor. I sorry you are upset. Lady and I want to play together. I promise I won't do it again. Sinserly, Bobby."

Mother agreed to deliver the letter in person. In retrospect, I realize it must have taken a lot of courage on her part.

A week later I received an invitation to Laddie Kadoo's fifth birthday party.

His First Haircut

For Reflection

And be kind to one another, tenderhearted, forgiving one another, as God in Christ has forgiven you (Eph. 4:32).

First experiences are memorable events and may well shape the way we view reality throughout our lives. The first experience of forgiveness is no exception.

When I shared "His First Haircut" with a study group, almost everyone came to the defense of the six-year-old who had cut his friend's hair. "He didn't mean to do harm. Laddie agreed to have his hair cut. It was an innocent childhood mistake." The one exception was a mother whose own five-year-old had her Shirley Temple curls removed by neighborhood girls playing "Beauty Parlor"!

The fact of the matter is that many of the hurts of life are caused by those who don't realize what they are doing or the harm that they are causing. Yet so much of the pain of life is perpetrated in just this way—thoughtlessly, but without malice.

The young boy of this story learned many things from his first experience: taking responsibility for his own behavior, finding a way to say "I'm sorry," making amends where possible, being restored to relationship through forgiveness.

You may want to reflect on some of your own first experiences of forgiveness. What did you learn? What lessons do you still have to learn? What helped forgiveness and reconciliation to take place? What hindered them?

You might want to look at your present relationships. Are there any that could be helped by saying, "I'm sorry"? Are there people you need to forgive? Are there people who have been reaching out to you and to whom you haven't responded, whose desire for reconciliation you have ignored?

We have erred and stayed from thy ways like lost sheep....We have done those things which we ought not to have done. —The Book of Common Prayer

His First Haircut

The Accident

When I arrived as rector of St. Catherine's, they were still talking about The Accident. Nine months had passed since Greg had been killed in a tragic car wreck, but conversations on the church lawn and in almost every house I visited during those first weeks in my first parish eventually came around to the subject of Greg—and Norm.

Greg was the son of one of the founding families of St. Catherine's. So was Norm. Both families had been on the congregation's original mission board and, later, on the vestry of the new parish. They had vacationed together, played canasta together, and, of course, knelt next to each other at the altar rail. Norm and Greg had been among the first Sunday school kids in the church and, when they grew a little older, they were altar boys together. Their parents called them the "book ends," referring to the fact that they knelt at opposite ends of the altar; from where their parents knelt in the congregation, the boys appeared to be propping up the Lord's table.

The accident occurred when the two boys were seventeen years old and juniors in high school. It was a Friday night and it was raining. Norm was driving, Greg was in the front passenger seat, and three friends were in the back seat. They had been to a movie. For some reason, Greg had rolled down the window on the passenger side and stuck his head out into the weather to catch the fresh rain on his tongue. The car hit an oil slick, slid out of control, and rolled over into a ditch overflowing with water. Greg died that night. Norm and the other passengers were barely scratched.

In the investigation that followed, it was determined that Greg's body had been partially thrown out of the car. His head had been wedged between the roof of the car and the bottom of the ditch. His neck had been broken. The other boys stated that they had tried to free Greg from the wreckage but couldn't move the car.

When the police arrived at the scene, the four survivors were standing at the edge of the ditch and staring down, almost paralyzed. Norm was crying softly. Police tests indicated no alcohol in the blood stream of any of the boys. A charge of involuntary manslaughter was, nevertheless, brought against Norm. Weeks later he appeared before the circuit court judge in Duval County, Florida. The judge ruled that it was an accident and dismissed the charges.

Both Norm's parents and Greg's were in the court room. There was much hugging when the judge's gavel fell, bringing the proceedings to an end.

Everyone expressed joy and relief—except Norm, who just stood there without any visible sign of emotion.

As the families walked out to the municipal parking lot, Greg's father stopped Norm before he got into his car. He put a hand on each of Norm's shoulders and tried to make eye contact with him.

" Norm," he said, Greg's mother and I have forgiven you, the judge has forgiven you, God has forgiven you. Please, Norm for Greg's sake, forgive yourself."

Norm cried for the first time since the night of the accident.

The Accident

For Reflection

Therefore I tell you, people will be forgiven for every sin and blasphemy, but blasphemy against the Spirit will not be forgiven (Mt. 12:31).

We can do nothing so terrible that God can't forgive us. That is important to remember. That is the good news of the Christian faith. Unfortunately, we often ignore what we have been taught about God's willingness to forgive, and are fascinated with the idea of " an unforgivable sin."

If we have any conscience at all, we fall too easily into the trap of judging ourselves more harshly than anybody else does. What a nightmare of self-accusation Norm must have endured. " If only...if only we had stayed home that night. If only I had taken the main highway instead of the river road. If only...."

Sometimes we convince ourselves that our sin is so bad that even a loving God cannot forgive us. Jesus may have died on the cross for the sins of the whole world, but he didn't die to forgive _____ and _____ and _____.

The unforgivable sin, or the sin against the Holy Spirit, might be described in just this way: God cannot do what we refuse to let him do, which is to forgive us for _____ and _____ and _____.

Or, if we have become so morally confused as to believe that good is evil and evil is good, then we are unable to receive forgiveness because we are unable to ask for it.

Almighty and everlasting God, you are always more ready to hear than we to pray, and to give more than we either desire or deserve: Pour upon us the abundance of your mercy, forgiving us those things of which our conscience is afraid, and giving us those good things for which we are not worthy to ask, ex-

cept through the merits and mediation of Jesus Christ our Savior; who lives and reigns with you and the Holy Spirit, one God, for ever and ever. —The Book of Common Prayer

Spenkelink's Priest

More than a decade ago now, when national attention focused on Starke, Florida, for John Spenkelink's execution, it revealed the work of a tall Episcopal priest fulfilling the biblical imperative to minister to those in prison.

Spenkelink was the first man to be executed against his will in the United States since 1967. Shortly after midnight on May 23, 1979, when word came that Supreme Court Justice Thurgood Marshall had granted Spenkelink an eleventh-hour stay of execution, the Rev. Tom Feamster emerged grinning from Spenkelink's Death Row cell block to express gratitude for one bit of hope momentarily being extended to the condemned man whom he now considered a friend.

Feamster and Spenkelink had been watching television together when news of the stay flashed on the screen—just seven hours before the time scheduled for the execution. "John took a deep breath, and so did I. Suddenly I became very tired. Then he asked to receive Holy Communion."

A former pro-football player with the Baltimore Colts, in 1979 Feamster was vicar of St. Anne's Episcopal Church, Keystone Heights, Florida. He had been helping with communions at Florida's four state correctional institutions for several years. He had met John Spenkelink in 1977 when Governor Bob Graham first signed Spenkelink's death warrant. "I offered to visit with him then. He was getting a lot of unsolicited mail of a religious nature telling him how bad he was and how he was going to hell. Even the wizard of the KKK wrote him a letter.

"We started to have some good talks and John began to hear about forgiveness and grace. He knew how bad he was, but he had never heard that God loved him.

"I can assure you," Feamster continued, "John was not the same man who had committed that crime (six years before). That's part of the injustice of our system of capital punishment. God gives life and God will take life away. Our mission is to preach the Good News enabling people to change their lives. When we snuff out a life, that precludes us from doing any kind of ministry.

"John didn't fear dying, but he was very much into life. He no longer felt money was important. He was beginning to learn about the real values of life. He was interested in dealing with people. He would have been a productive member of society, whether he was in prison or not."

During his six years in prison, Spenkelink was disciplined only twice. Once he held onto his tray when the guards took away personal privileges. He was knocked unconscious and sustained a broken rib.

By November 1978, Spenkelink was ready to receive communion, but couldn't. The prison superintendent had put up a wall so the twenty-nine Death Row inmates who had completed the appeal process could no longer have any personal contact with the outside world. "I had to speak to him through a mike," stated Feamster. After a plea to the governor's office, Feamster obtained permission to take communion to Spenkelink during his last days.

"During one of our private sessions, John wanted to pray for the governor. I wanted to tell the press about this, but he wouldn't let me. He thought that it would be misunderstood. He just didn't hate the man. He forgave him and said he loved him."

Spenkelink asked Feamster to be one of the witnesses to his execution. "He wanted to look out and see a friendly face." Feamster read the fifth chapter of Matthew (the Sermon on the Mount) while he waited in the viewing room. "It was one of his favorites."

The press reported a look of terror in the condemned man's eyes as the hood was lowered over his face. "I think they misinterpreted the data," stated Feamster. "The straps were so tight he could hardly breathe. His eyes were bulging out."

Reporters also noted that Spenkelink wasn't allowed to make the traditional final statement. Feamster said, "I'm not sure he wanted to. When we were having communion at 7:55 a.m. on the day of his death, he wrote across the back page of my prayer book, "Human beings are just what they let themselves be. He who says he loves God and hates his neighbor is a liar! I feel myself as being a little bit of a thing just by being human...but a real one."

On the Saturday following John Spenkelink's execution, seventy-five inmates gathered for prayer and fellowship. It was reported that things were very quiet that morning. There was a deep sense of loss. The men prayed for their brother and for his family. "There was much love in that small Christian fellowship," one of them said.

There are still over one hundred men on Florida's death row.

For Reflection

"Jesus, remember me when you come into your kingdom." He replied, "Truly I tell you, today you will be with me in Paradise" (Lk. 23:42-43).

Those who have ministered in prisons tell me that the inmates are encouraged by the fact that many of the major biblical figures they know about have "done time" in jail. The fact that men like Joseph, Daniel, John the Baptist, Paul, and Jesus had at some point not only lost their physical freedom, but also experienced the indignities that go with incarceration, is a point of contact.

Of particular comfort to these prisoners is Luke's story of the thief on the cross. Although Luke's account does not give the man a name, tradition knows him as Dismas, and there are many prison chapels dedicated to St. Dismas.

The message of the thief's brief encounter with Jesus is a clear and simple one: it is never too late to turn to the Lord. Even at the last minute, he hears us and responds in love that opens the door to his kingdom. The same point is made in the parable of the Laborers in the Vineyard (Mt. 20:1-16).

Think about God's unconditional love for us. Think about the fact that God never gives up on us, even when we may have given up on ourselves. How do you feel about this kind of forgiveness? Is there anybody you know who you would rather *not* have God forgive at the last minute?

An elder was asked by a certain soldier if God would forgive a sinner. And he said to him: Tell me, beloved, if your cloak is torn, will you throw it away? The soldier replied and said: No. I will mend it and put it back on. The elder said to him: If you take care of your cloak, will God not be merciful to His own image? —The Sayings of the Desert Fathers

Spenkelink's Priest

He Will Understand It Better

My wife, Lynne, and I were in Virginia Beach for the annual art festival. When it began to rain, we retreated, along with our friends Jim and Sara Samuel, to our recreational vehicle parked at the edge of the boardwalk. Jim preceded me as chaplain at Episcopal High School and had just returned to the States following a three-year assignment at the American Church in Weisbaden, Germany.

We brought the Samuels up to date on the events in our lives, talked about mutual friends, and then listened to their tales of overseas adventure. Jim's church in Wiesbaden, St. Augustine of Canterbury, had originally been a Church of England chaplaincy for the city's English-speaking business community prior to World War I. Because Weisbaden ended up in the U.S. sector of the post-World War II division of Germany, and because of its proximity to U.S. military installations, St. Augustine's came under the jurisdiction of the Episcopal Church of the United States.

"Do you have any Germans in your congregation?" I asked.

"Not many," Jim said. "But every other week, Martin Niemoller comes to church."

Martin Niemoller! That name made my head spin. Martin Niemoller and Dietrich Bonhoeffer had been the great heroes of my church history class in seminary because of their resistance to Hitler. On top of that, I had just found, in a used bookstore, an old magazine in which Niemoller was featured. On the cover of the December 23, 1940 issue of *Time* was a portrait of Pastor Niemoller in his distinctive clerical garb. Behind his head, in red, was a cross and a swastika. The headline on the cover read, "Martyrs of 1940. In Germany only the cross has not bowed to the swastika," while the feature article on Niemoller reported that as the second Christmas of Hitler's war in Europe approached, between 200,000 and 800,000 people were behind barbed wire in Germany. At that point eighty percent of the prisoners in the concentration camps were Christians. Before he could attack the Jews, Hitler had to control or at least neutralize the Christians.

Albert Einstein, a Jew and an agnostic, attested to the strength of the Christian resistance symbolized by Niemoller's imprisonment. "Being a lover of freedom, when the revolution came in Germany," Einstein recalled, "I looked to the universities to defend it, knowing that they had always boasted of their devotion to the cause of truth; but, no, the universities immediately were silenced. Then I looked to the great editors of the newspapers whose flaming editorials in days gone by had proclaimed their love of freedom; but they like the universities were silenced in a few short weeks. Only the Church stood squarely across the path of Hitler's campaign for suppressing truth. I never had any special interest in the Church before, but now I feel a great affection and admiration because the Church alone has had the courage and persistence to stand for intellectual truth and moral freedom. I am forced thus to confess that what I once despised, I now praise unreservedly."

By 1940 many monasteries in Germany were closed, Roman Catholic priests were expelled from their parishes or forbidden to preach, many Protestant seminary graduates were refused ordination, and vocal young priests and pastors were drafted into the army as privates and sent to the Russian front. Despite this campaign, there emerged a strong and outspoken religious group in Germany known as the Confessing Church, which declared, "Our bishop and council remain the legal authority of our church...The Lord of the Christian Church is Christ, not Hitler."

Pastor Niemoller, a former submarine commander and holder of the Iron Cross from World War I, would put the position of many German Christians even more bluntly: "Not you, Herr Hitler, but God is my Fuhrer."

Niemoller was arrested and confined in a series of concentration camps, but he was not silenced completely. In time for Christmas 1940, his message reached the United States: "There is one thing I want to ask of you all, that we give no place to weariness, to capitulation! There are those who would persuade us that the suffering of our Church is a sign that it follows a perverted way. To that we reply confidently that the Apostles have borne witness to the contrary...In their strength let us go forward on the way—in His footsteps—unconcerned with the censure of men, but with the peace of Christ in our hearts and with praise of God on our lips. So help us God!"

In 1945, Allied troops found Niemoller alive when they liberated the prisoners at Dachau. In postwar Germany, Niemoller was a leader in rebuilding the Protestant churches. One of his first endeavors was to author a confession or "declaration of guilt by the German Churches for not opposing Hitler more strenuously."

Jim and I traded stories and bits of information we had about the famous old man, now in his late eighties, who appeared every other Sunday in Jim's church with his much younger American wife.

"Their agreement is that they will go to a German church one week and come to us on alternate Sundays," Jim was told when he first learned of Niemoller's identity. Jim felt threatened, inadequate, and awed—all at the same time. "How will I ever preach the gospel of God's love and forgiveness to a man like Niemoller?" he asked someone in the congregation.

"He will understand it better than anyone else," was the reply.

For Reflection

Since all have sinned and fall short of the glory of God, they are now justified by his grace as a gift, through the redemption that is in Christ Jesus (Rom. 3:23-24).

When I finish telling God about the harmful things that I have done, "that I ought not to have done," I come to a tougher list—the things "I have left undone." On a slow day, I may come up with a near-perfect score on the first section, but I never seem to get a clean bill of health on the second. A day never passes when I could not have done more.

This is part of the paradox of being a Christian. We become increasingly more sensitive to the needs of those around us and at the same time more aware of God's love and grace and forgiveness as an unearned, unmerited gift.

A parishioner who is a new Christian confesses, "I've driven down that street a thousand times and I have never before noticed all of the street people living in boxes under the bridge and interstate overpass." Some would label this as unhealthy wallowing in guilt; but Christians know better. It is the beginning of a Christian conscience. C. FitzSimmons Allison in his book *Guilt, Anger, and God* speaks of " O *felix culpa*, O happy guilt, the shadow of our humanity. When we walk in the light we cast a shadow. To see the shadow of our guilt is just the negative way of saying the light is still on!"

I marvel at the paradox of Pastor Martin Niemoller, fresh out of prison and coming forward to share the guilt of the German churches for not doing more to oppose Hitler more strenuously. What more could he have done? What more could the churches have done? Only God knows. The point is, it is important to ask the question.

We always need to ask, Am I doing enough? Could I have done more? Is my church doing enough? Is my local, state, or federal government doing enough?

Do I not share some responsibility for the social evils which I see, hear about and read about daily? Have I always used my opportunities as a citizen to relieve suffering, to speak out against injustice, to promote harmony in the life of my city, my country, and the nations of the world? —Liturgy for the Day of Atonement, Reform Tradition

Why Don't You Turn It Over to God?

"Come out and see what's left of me," said the husky voice at the other end of the phone. "Stay about an hour. An hour is about all I can take of you," she chuckled.

It was the fall of 1975 and I was in San Antonio, Texas, for a meeting. About all the time I had was an hour before my plane would head back east. The whiskey tenor voice on the other end of the line was that of Gertrude Behanna. Writing under the pen name of Elizabeth Burns in her book *The Late Liz,* Gert had told her story of a pampered childhood at the Waldorf-Astoria Hotel, her education at Smith College, three marriages, bouts with alcohol and drugs, attempted suicide, and conversion to Christianity. In her words, "I used benzedrine to get me up, alcohol to keep me up, and sleeping pills to get me to bed. (Pause) That made for a very short day." After its publication in the mid-fifties, she made her witness personally to thousands, perhaps millions, of people for the next twenty years.

Our paths first crossed when she was writing her book in Twentynine Palms, California. I was a young Marine officer with a pregnant wife. Gert lived in a pink stucco house on top of a hill overlooking the reactivated Marine base and the oasis from which the settlement took its name. (I could count only nineteen palm trees). Gert's house served as the gathering place for a little church congregation that met under the leadership of a Church Army captain, John Hunt.

Up to that point in my life, church had meant stained glass windows, pews, robed choir, and a pipe organ. This was my first experience of church as community.

We would stumble through Morning Prayer, about twenty of us sitting around on the available chairs and kneeling on the carpet. One Sunday when we thought we were through, Captain Hunt remembered that he had forgotten to recite the psalm, so we backed up, and among muffled snickers we proceeded to do our duty to the Psalter. Then having handled our "bounden duty and service" in a proper fashion, decently and in order, we were ready for the coffee hour.

"Before you get up," said a deep voice coming from a small woman with a monkey face, "please pray for Bill. They found him, thank God, and he's getting some treatment. He's been sober for five days now." Gert was referring to one of her two sons. One was a priest, the other an alcoholic.

As it turned out, this was to be one of Bill's many recoveries. Gert later confessed that Bill's real sobriety didn't begin until she decided she loved him so much that she wasn't going to keep bailing him out to satisfy her own guilt. As often happens with alcoholics, Bill had fallen off the wagon one Christmas. Gert got word that he was in jail; and as she drove across the desert to see him, she prayed that she would have the strength and courage to do the loving thing for Bill. As it turned out the loving thing was also a most painful experience. Gert refused to post bail and told Bill why. He burst into tears. She got up and left his cell. He screamed out, "Mother, Mother, don't leave me here." The metal door was closed. "Like Lot's wife," says Gert, "I made the mistake of looking back. There was a Christmas wreath on the door and it framed Bill's face. I heard him crying all the way back to Twentynine Palms."

Since my wife and I were the youngest couple in the congregation, Gert and the little church surrounded us with their love. Although she had a 3 x 5 filecard tacked to her door saying "I'm a writer and will not answer the door or phone before four in the afternoon," she gave me strict instructions. "When the baby comes, throw rocks at my window no matter what time is it. Make them small rocks."

Our son John was born at the local hospital at five in the morning. I had donned a surgical gown and had been with his mother during the delivery. The doctor complimented me on being "Mr. Cool" during the whole procedure, but when it was all over, I went back to my wife's room and wept tears of joy and relief for ten minutes. When they sent me home at day break, I headed across the desert road to Gert's. At noon the desert is a dull, flat beige; but at daybreak it sparkles with color, or so it seemed on that first day of my son's life. Gert's head shot out the window at the first pebble. "A man child, how wonderful. Come on up. I'll fix you some breakfast, Lieutenant. You've put in a hard night." It was a natural to ask Gert to be John's godmother at the baptism that took place in her living room two months later.

The Late Liz was a long time in writing. I had been discharged from the Marines, entered seminary, and been ordained by the time it was finally published. The literary world took little note, but, like Gert, her book was a late bloomer, eventually selling over a million copies. "It was the sexy paperback cover that did it," she was fond of saying. "Those heavy breathers looking for some light reading didn't expect to get a story about God's love."

Eventually the speaking invitations began to come in. In 1961, when I was rector of St. Catherine's, Jacksonville, I heard that she would be in Atlanta. When I phoned an invitation Gert responded, "Listen, sweetie, I can't leave Atlanta before two, Saturday afternoon, and I have to be in Charlotte by six on Sunday night. If you can work that out with the airlines I'll consider it a direct order from God."

An order it was. The scheduled departure and arrival times were within five minutes of her specifications. She spoke to a packed church on Saturday night and at two crowded services the next day. The bishop issued her an invitation to return to the diocese for a month the following year.

One of Gert's close friends, Helen Plummer, who came down for the event, confessed to me, " Gert gives me too much credit for her conversion. She tells everyone I said, 'Gert, why don't you turn it all over to God?'. What I actually said was, 'Gert, why don't you turn it all over to God, or I'll turn you over to the police.'"

But Gert heard what God wanted her to hear. " I felt cleansed, welcomed, and forgiven, and I knew exactly who this was....Something had been added to my life—a plus—a plus in the shape of the cross. When someone asked, 'My God, what's happened to you?' I replied, 'My God has happened to me.'"

Even though she was near seventy during her speaking tour, Gert had a special appeal to teenagers and college kids. Her statement, "The only reason I'm here is because two thousand years ago a very gracious young man named Jesus Christ said do this," had the simplicity and directness few could resist.

All this and a thousand other memories raced across my private video screen as I waited on that day in 1975 for the door to her San Antonio apartment to open.

We hugged. "Gert, you look the same as you did when I first met you."

"Sweetie," she replied, "I was old then and I'm still old."

She was eighty-one, and weighed a hundred and four pounds. Her hair was still short and showing only flecks of gray—"I don't have to fuss over it that way." She had had several operations on her eyes and was adjusting to bifocals. "God doesn't ask you to bear too much at one time. He says, 'Hold off on Gert's arthritis for a while, we've got to let her take care of the eyes'" We reminisced about her visits to Florida; I brought her up to date on John and told her about my marriage to Lynne. She would be moving to Minnesota soon. Her son, the Rev. Bard Smith, a professor at Carlton College, was building an apartment onto his house for Gert.

It was a short hour. The taxi arrived. We hugged each other. We both knew, but didn't say, that our paths might not cross again. We said a prayer together and hugged again.

When word came a year later of her death on December 8, 1976, it was accompanied by a note from her son Bard.

On the day before her death, a young black man had been baptized in Gert's apartment. After the baptism, Gert said to him, "Mark, you know what's just happened? No longer can you or I define ourselves by the color of our skin or who our parents are, what we own or where we've been, but simply by our relationship to Jesus Christ. Mark, you are now my brother."

60

Bard wrote, "Those were practically Mother's last words."

For Reflection
You gave me no kiss, but from the time I came in she has not stopped kissing my feet. You did not anoint my head with oil, but she has anointed my feet with ointment. Therefore, I tell you, her sins, which were many, have been forgiven; hence she has shown great love. But the one to whom little is forgiven, loves little (Lk. 7:45-47).

Anyone who ever listened to Gert Behanna speak, or talked to her for more than ten minutes, came away with the strong impression that here was someone who had experienced God's unconditional love, unconditional forgiveness, and unconditional acceptance. There was nothing phony about Gert. She was, in many ways, like the woman who interrupted the dinner party and bathed Jesus' feet in Luke's gospel. She had been forgiven much and so could love much.

Tradition has sometimes identified the woman at the dinner party with Mary of Magda (Mary Magdalene). While there is nothing in the biblical text to support this theory, the two characters had a similar experience of Jesus' unconditional love.

People like Gert and Mary Magdalene make a lot of people just a little bit jealous. They obviously are enjoying their Christianity a lot more than most of us. Could the key to their joy be in their willingness to turn it over to God? Ask yourself, have I really turned my life over to the Lord? If not, what part am I holding back?

And here we offer and present unto thee, O Lord, our selves, our souls and bodies, to be a reasonable,

holy, and living sacrifice unto thee. —The Book of
Common Prayer

Where Does an Unwed Father Find a Home?

Forty years ago, divorce among the clergy was either unheard of or became the occasion for 36-point headlines in the tabloid press. The erring or abandoned cleric vacated the parsonage under cover of darkness, never to be heard of again except as a tragic figure in a Tennessee Williams play.

In the spring of 1973, the fact that things were changing came home to me in a very dramatic way. On April Fool's Day, after twenty years, three days, and four children, I was told that my marriage was over. Bishops, priests, friends, counselors, and inlaws couldn't change the course of events. Legal maneuvering and challenges on my part delayed but did not prevent the inevitable. On November 23, 1973, after two court appearances, the decree was final.

My bishop canceled his appointments and sat in court with me. The dean of our cathedral insisted that I celebrate Holy Communion at the cathedral altar on the Sunday following my final court appearance. From the end of August until the final decree, I accepted the hospitality of the old archdeacon, Fred Yerkes, who lived in his family home which had not changed since his childhood in the early 1900s. A fireplace supplied the heat and the plumbing was primitive. It was, nevertheless, what I needed—a safe haven. Fred was a good listener, but he never pried, never played amateur psychiatrist. I called his house "Uncle Freddy's Home for Unwed Fathers."

Everyone I have ever known who has experienced a divorce likens it to a death experience. Some even say it is worse than death. Certainly I was no exception. I went through the stages of denial, bargaining, anger, and depression before I could come to a point of acceptance and rebuilding. For instance, on the night of the final decree, I bought a quart of Scotch, rented an oceanfront room at the Holiday Inn, and sat on the balcony drinking and contemplating a dramatic dive into the pool five stories below.

The court had ordered the sale of our house and the profits were to be divided. When the family moved out, I moved back in.

On the first day back in the house, I was beginning the cleanup process when I became aware of someone else in the house. I tiptoed up the stairs to find a little guy of no more than four busily inspecting the empty bedrooms. He picked up the remnant of a broken toy. " Do you have a little boy?"

" Yes," I replied.

" Where's his bed?"

" It's gone."

" Gone—he doesn't sleep here?"

" No, he doesn't sleep here."

" Where's the Mommy?"

" She's gone."

" Oh. Is she coming back?"

" I don't know."

" Oh "

He headed down the stairs and stopped at the front door.

" Everybody ought to have a mommy," he said and headed down the street. I'd tell you his name, but I had never seen him before nor have I seen him since.

But the pain was more than loneliness. I felt had failed at life's most important endeavor. I was

Where Does an Unwed Father Find a Home?

ashamed. If the root meaning of the Hebrew word for sin is, as I learned in seminary, "missing the mark," then my life was way off target. If sin had to do with broken relationships, then mine was in little pieces, all over the landscape, for all to see. If we are responsible not only for the things that we have done but also for the things we have left undone, then I was guilty—or at least I felt guilty. And even though I had not sought the divorce, I knew that I was responsible in part for the failure of the marriage.

Add to that the vocational crisis. I wondered if I could, in fact, continue to be a priest, or if I should quietly look for some other form of employment. My position as director of development at the Jacksonville Episcopal High School was not put in jeopardy by my domestic crisis, and as an associate of the cathedral, I continued to perform liturgical functions at least two Sundays a month. The little mission congregation of St. Margaret's on the St. John's River, which I had taken under my wing on occasional weekends, refused to hear of my resignation. But even with such official support, I wondered if I could continue as a priest. Did I have anything to offer and, most important of all, could I forgive myself for what had happened?

The answer to my questions came on the feast of the Epiphany, January 6, 1974. It was a beautiful day. In the morning, I preached at the 11:00 service at the cathedral. My oldest son, John, met me for lunch and an afternoon of golf. Then I rushed back to the still unsold house to meet friends, Henry and Mary Hoyt, for a dinner date. Henry's instructions to me had been, "Mary and I will pick you up at 6:30 and take you out to the beach for dinner."

I had just stepped out of the shower when the doorbell rang. Barefoot, in slacks and a tee shirt, I opened the front door. There stood Henry and Mary and behind them were seventy or eighty members of my former parish, St. Catherine's. People swarmed everywhere. Folding tables were placed in the garage; metal chairs appeared all over the patio. "We're having a parish supper," said one matron as she placed a platter of potato salad on the table.

When supper was over, the senior warden announced, "That's not all!" A pile, then a mound, and then a mountain of gifts began to grow on the patio.

"We're giving you a shower," said Mary Alice Chalker. "Your mother said you didn't have a pot to put flowers in, so we've bought you some pots and a few other things you'll need."

There were eggbeaters, measuring cups, dish towels, grits, and toilet paper but mostly, there was a lot of love. I looked around with blurred vision at the folks who had come that night. I had known most of them for more than ten years. I knew a lot about the pain that was in some of their lives and I had been allowed to share in it; now they were sharing in mine. I felt accepted and forgiven, and found that I could now forgive myself, too.

For Reflection

Jesus said to them again, "Peace be with you. As the Father has sent me, so I send you." When he had said this, he breathed on them and said to them, "Receive the Holy Spirit. If you forgive the sins of any, they are forgiven them; if you retain the sins of any, they are retained" (Jn. 20:21-23).

Jesus was criticized by the religious leaders of his day for claiming the authority to forgive sins. He further enraged his critics by passing on that authority to his church, as it is recorded in the passage

66

from the Fourth Gospel cited above. It is with this apostolic authority that the clergy pronounce the "absolution" or forgiveness of sins to a congregation or to an individual.

I would like to add that in a very real sense, the gift of forgiveness and reconciliation was given to the whole Christian community and not just to the clergy. This certainly has been my own experience. The community of the church, through the bishop and the dean, "forgave" me the failure of my marriage and said that I could continue to function as a priest. But it was the ministry of the laity of my former parish who were the reconciling and healing agents empowering me and enabling me to continue.

The Christian communities in which we live play a vital role in the business of forgiveness. No matter what the Bible says, and no matter what the bishop pronounces, it is the community that forgives the sinner and receives him or her back into fellowship or "retains the sin" and closes the door on the sinner.

The gospel story of the raising of Lazarus has some application here (Jn. 11:1-44). Jesus brought Lazarus back to life, but it was the community that was given the job of unbinding him.

You may want to reflect on the life of the community in which you live. Is it a forgiving, reconciling community which will receive back the individual who has missed the mark? How could your community be more forgiving? More loving? More an instrument of reconciliation?

Lord, make us instruments of your peace. Where there is hatred, let us sow love; where there is injury, pardon; where there is discord, union; where there is doubt, faith; where there is despair, hope; where

*there is darkness, light; where there is sadness, joy;
Grant that we may not so much seek to be consoled as
to console; to be understood as to understand; to be
loved as to love. For it is in giving that we receive; it is
in pardoning that we are pardoned; and it is in dying
that we are born to eternal life.* —Prayer of St. Francis
of Assisi

I Love Idi Amin

When the list of the top ten tyrants of the twentieth century is finally compiled, Idi Amin of Uganda may not make the final cut. After all, there have been so many. But throughout the 1970s his name was a household word, synonymous with brutality and political oppression.

Like so many dictators, Amin first came to power with a broad base of hopeful popular support. Festo Kivengere, the Anglican bishop of Kigezi Diocese in Uganda, recalls returning home after Amin's January 25, 1971 coup that deposed the oppressive Milton Obote: "There was indeed great enthusiasm as the new head of state promised to hold free elections...political prisoners were being released...he even urged all Ugandans to be faithful in worship at their church or mosque."

In Uganda, a country of eleven million people, some seven million are Christians. Of that number, over three million are Anglicans. The new political order received the prayers and enthusiastic support of the church, which had been planted only a century before by the missionary movement in Africa.

Sadly, the political honeymoon in Uganda was short. The military were given extraordinary power. Leaders, including a member of the country's Supreme Court, began to disappear. The churches raised their voices and paid a high price as they approached the one hundredth anniversary of the coming of Christianity to Uganda.

In the calendars of both the Anglican and Roman Catholic churches, the Martyrs of Uganda are remembered. A monument to them, visited by both the Pope and the Archbishop of Canterbury, stands near the sports stadium in Kampala. When the first missionaries of the Church of England brought Christianity to Uganda in 1877, they were welcomed by King Kabaka Mutesa. The king invited young Christians to serve at his court as pages. However, the king's son, Kabaka Mwanga, a Muslim, was suspicious of the English Christians and decided, for both political and religious reasons, to get rid of them.

Bishop Hannington, an Anglican, was murdered. The king's three Christian pages, ranging in age from eleven to fifteen, were arrested and sentenced to death by fire. The execution also involved severing the condemned boys' arms so they didn't thrash around too much. As the boys died, they sang "Tukutendereza Yesu," now known as "The Martyrs' Song." One verse says, "O that I had wings like the angels, I would fly away and be with Jesus." The youngest page, Yusufu, was said to have pleaded with the executioner, "Please don't cut off my arms. I will not struggle in the fire that takes me to Jesus!" Tradition has it that many who witnessed the martyrdom of the Ugandan boys became Christians.

History was to repeat itself early in 1977. A large centenary rally marking the coming of Christianity to Uganda was being planned for the sports stadium in Kampala. Six young actors who were going to play the roles of the Martyrs of Uganda were found massacred together in a field—not far from the Martyrs' memorial. Uganda's Anglican archbishop, Janani Luwum, a critic of Amin's oppression, met the same fate as Bishop Hannington.

I Love Idi Amin

This was the political climate in Uganda when Bishop Festo Kivengere sought asylum in London. He had been with his friend Archbishop Luwum on February 16, 1977, the day Luwum was summoned to meet Idi Amin. The next day Kivengere heard a radio report that Luwum had been killed in an automobile accident. Kivengere got word that his own name was also on Idi Amin's "list." He crossed the Ugandan border on February 20 and arrived in London the following month.

When Bishop Kivengere visited Jacksonville, Florida, in 1978 to conduct a diocesan teaching and preaching mission, he spoke of the bitterness and grief he had continued to carry with him in exile in London. He knew that his hatred was affecting his ministry, for he realized that he could not preach about the love of God and at the same time carry the hatred—however justified—he felt for Idi Amin.

" I had to face my own attitude toward President Amin and his agents," Kivengere told us in Jacksonville. " The Holy Spirit showed me I was getting hard in my spirit, and that my hardness and bitterness toward those who were persecuting us could only bring spiritual loss. This would take away my ability to communicate the love of God, which is the essence of my ministry and testimony.

" So I had to ask for forgiveness from the Lord, and for grace to love President Amin more, because these events had shaken my loving relationship with all those people. God gave me the assurance of forgiveness on Good Friday, when I was in a congregation that sat for three hours in All Souls' Church in London, meditating on the redeeming love of Jesus Christ. Right there the Lord healed me...This was fresh air for my tired soul. I knew I had seen the Lord and been released: love filled my heart."

The words, "Father forgive," had special meaning for Kivengere. "God used that sentence to open my heart. Quietly, I entered into a deeper liberation, and I went home to my wife, breathing the fresh air."

When Bishop Kivengere got back to his apartment, he told his wife what had happened at All Souls. He said that he could not only forgive, but could actually *love* Idi Amin.

Late in 1977, Kivengere would write, "We look back with great love to our country. We love President Idi Amin. We owe him the debt of love, for he is one of those for whom Christ shed His precious blood. As long as he is still alive, he is still redeemable. Pray for him, that in the end he may see a new way of life, rather than a way of death."

Bishop Kivengere was able to return to his homeland following Amin's overthrow on April 11, 1979, and continued his ministry in Uganda until his death in 1988. Amin who gained political asylum in Saudi Arabia—was still alive in 1991 at the age of sixty-six.

For Reflection

For mortals it is impossible, but for God all things are possible (Mt. 19:26).

Like many of us, Bishop Kivengere was confronted with a clear-cut decision. He could understandably and justifiably hold onto all the pain and resentment of the past. Such a decision carried with it a price: if he continued to hate, he would be unable to love. If he spoke of resentment and revenge, he would be unable to speak of redemption and salvation.

I wish I could have a recording of the thoughts that went on in his brain on that Good Friday in London. Somehow the message of the cross got through to him as never before. If Jesus could forgive those who had crucified him, then perhaps it would be possible for Bishop Kivengere to forgive Idi Amin. On a human level such a decision is close to impossible, but the evidence in this story is that with God all things are possible, even forgiving and loving one's enemies.

What do we learn from that man on the cross? What do we learn from the experience of Bishop Kivengere and others like him? When we hold onto the old hatreds, they continue to have power over us. When we let them go, when we turn them over to God, we are free to become the loving persons God intended us to be.

One of the elders was asked what was humility, and he said: If you forgive a brother who has injured you before he himself asks pardon. —The Sayings of the Desert Fathers

" The Rape of the Vicarage Virgin"

Please forgive the title. It wasn't my idea at all. It was the headline in one of London's many daily tabloids—publications that make our supermarket checkout counter weeklies look like sober Victorian novels by comparison.

The vicarage in question is a nondescript post-World War II Church of England parsonage, nestled behind the ancient Church of St. Mary's, whose first priest was instituted to this cure in the twelfth century. My wife and I had lived in St. Mary's vicarage for six weeks in the spring of 1984 when Michael Saward, the vicar, and I had exchanged parishes. He and his wife Jackie had lived in our rectory in Orange Park, Florida, while we occupied their home in a London suburb that, to our delight, was only thirty minutes by subway from London's West End theater district. We felt perfectly safe in the vicarage, although our nearest neighbors either occupied a row of pensioners flats or the booths and stools at the nearby Rose and Crown pub. We never had an uneasy moment, even late at night when we walked the narrow lane from the station to the vicarage.

But it was in broad daylight on a day in March that Michael got up from his study desk to answer the vicarage door bell. Before he had time to think, a man had a knife at his belly and, followed by two accomplices, had forced his way through the front hall and into his study. "Where's the safe? Where do you keep the money?" There was no safe and no money—save for the few pound notes and coins in Michael's pocket and in his desk drawer.

Michael's daughter Jill and her boyfriend David were quickly discovered by the accomplices in the living room and brought into the study.

"They had a knife to Jill's face," Michael said, "made David and me lie on the floor, and demanded of Jill, 'Where does your mother keep her jewelry?'"

"She doesn't have any jewelry," Jill said promptly, to which the intruder replied, "We'll see about that!" He led Jill, still at knife point, up the stairs to the second floor. Michael was to learn later that the men had already cut the telephone wires.

"At that point," Michael said, "there wasn't anything obviously sexual about the whole affair. It seemed like a robbery and nothing more—although I was concerned about the youngest of the three men, who seemed to be high on drugs or something else. Then, David and I were made to drop our trousers around our ankles and hobble up to the second floor and into the large bedroom where Jill was sitting naked on the bed. We were forced to lie down on the floor with our hands loosely tied, while the youngest of the men led Jill to one of the other bedrooms. Suddenly, I felt a tremendous crack on the head. Everything went yellow and black. I wondered if I had been shot; I decided to sham death. I drifted in and out of consciousness, and vaguely remember the intruders hitting and kicking David. Later, I discovered they had used my cricket bat as a weapon."

The next thing Michael remembers is the front door of the vicarage slamming. Then he realized Jill was standing at his side.

"Are you alright, Dad?"

"Have they gone?" Michael asked.

"Yes."

THE FORGIVENESS BOOK

"Jill, what about you?"

"What do you think?"

The story became front page news in Britain, not only in the tabloids and the *Times*; it was the lead story on the BBC and Independent Television news for several days. A massive police investigation followed and the three men were caught within a week. Jill, Michael, and David were questioned separately, and were warned not to discuss the details of the case with each other. "I knew that Jill had been raped," Michael said, "but I knew few of the details until almost a year later when the case came to trial at the Old Bailey."

The crime brought both a public outcry of indignation and an outpouring of love and sympathy for the victims. Thousands of letters and cards came to the vicarage from around the world. The Archbishop of Canterbury, the Prime Minister, and the leader of the Labour Party all sent personal messages, while the royal family expressed its concern through a personal visit by Princess Anne.

At this point what was one story becomes two—Michael's story and Jill's story.

Michael had been hospitalized for six days when BBC and Independent Television crews staged bedside interviews with him. Both channels ran the interviews in prime time. Michael was asked, among other things, if he could forgive the three men who had invaded his home. His reply set off a national debate: he could forgive what had been done to him, but he could not forgive what had been done to his daughter. Only Jill could do that. Her father could only express outrage and demand that justice be done.

"I cannot attempt to declare forgiveness on behalf of others. If Jill is able to forgive, then she must say

"The Rape of the Vicarage Virgin"

so. It is empty and wooly-minded for me to think that I can do it for her. My response should be anger at those who raped her and passionate concern for justice to be done to them by society's appointed arbitrators, the judges."

He drew a parallel between his own ability to forgive the Germans for the bombing of his London neighborhood in World War II. However, regarding the Holocaust, "I have no right to try to forgive on behalf of the Jewish people. They alone can do that if they wish."

He was willing to forgive the men who invaded his home, even though he fully appreciated that he had a real encounter with the "naked reality of evil."

"I start from the premise that, first, God who is good, 'so loved the world that he gave his only Son' and, second, that evil is real and 'all have sinned and fall short of the glory of God.' There is really no point in talking about forgiveness unless you believe in the fact of evil." As a fallen human being who is a Christian, Michael finds it impossible *not* to forgive. "I forgive those who burst into my vicarage because I, as a Christian, want to obey my master's injunction and follow his example." For Michael, forgiveness and justice go together. They are not incompatible.

Remembering the dramatic visit that Pope John Paul II had paid to his would-be assassin, I asked Michael if he would be willing to visit his assailants in prison. "I would if they wanted me to. Actually, the eldest of the men did ask for a visit. He was, however, appealing his sentence at the time and the police insisted that I wait until the appeal process had been completed. I wrote him to that effect and invited him to contact me later. His appeal failed. I haven't heard from him since then."

For Jill, the first Sunday after the assault was a nightmare. In England as in America, the identity of the victim is supposed to be protected, but when she walked out of the vicarage to go to church, the cameras started to click. There were even photographers hanging out the windows over a nearby pub. She couldn't remember having her picture taken so frequently in all of her life. She walked straight for the church gate. "Nothing was going to stop me from worshipping my God."

Jill's experience with the medical professionals at the local hospital was almost as bad as the rape itself. The doctor who examined her was insensitive both physically and emotionally. He seemed to be implying that it was her fault—that she had "asked for it."

"The examination was the final straw," said Jill. "I know it has to be done, that it is part and parcel of reporting rape. Could it not be done with a little more compassion? With more appreciation of what the woman being examined has already undergone?"

She came away from the rape with many fears. The prospect of AIDS, pregnancy, and venereal disease were eventually eliminated by medical tests. But even now she is frightened by big knives, uncomfortable around unknown men in confined areas, and uneasy when she is in an unfamiliar group of people and the topic of rape comes into the conversation. More than that, she felt soiled and unclean. Would anybody or could anybody love her, want her? When and if she got married, could she have normal sexual relations with her husband? Could she ever conceive and bear a child?

David, her boyfriend, had a fractured skull and suffered a great deal of nerve damage in one ear. He entered the hospital on the critical list, but was dis-

"The Rape of the Vicarage Virgin"

charged eight days later. David's father and mother took them both to Scotland for a weekend's rest, and during the weekend, David proposed.

Jill was amazed, and flattered to find that someone still wanted her, even though she felt so unclean, but ultimately she decided not to marry him. One of the toughest decisions of her life was to tell him three months later that it couldn't be. She cared about him, and was grateful to him, but realized she could not allow their experience of the rape to be the thing that kept them together.

"Some acquaintances," said Jill, "treated me as though I'd developed some deformity." Her friends didn't always know how to handle the situation, either. They were stunned. "At first, they didn't know whether to mention the rape or not. I usually had to be the one who broke the ice. But it was still good that they were there when I needed them."

The turning point in Jill's recovery came on a weekend at a familiar youth camp in Wales. All by herself, she walked toward a cliff and actually contemplated throwing herself off it, into the sea below. She was tired, exhausted, and alone.

Her mind and spirit were engaged in the battle of her life. God had always comforted her before. Where was he now? He had given her life. Did she have the right to take it? Did she have the strength left to go on living? Her mind rambled and she stumbled toward the cliff.

"Oh, God," she cried, "if you want me to go on living, you'll have to give me the energy...the strength."

She heard some voices from the hill behind her. Some fellow campers were calling her name. She turned to see who they were. She wanted to run to them, but she was too tired; and yet she was no longer walking toward the sea.

Michael attributed his daughter's recovery to two factors: she was able to forgive her assailants and, at the same time, she was determined to do everything within her power to see that they were captured and convicted.

Her decision to forgive them came out of an earlier experience of wrestling with her understanding of the Lord's Prayer, and an old hurt that she had carried about for many years. Three years later she was able to write down her thoughts about forgiveness in a book she called *Rape: My Story*. " 'Forgive us our sins, as we forgive those who sin against us.' That's straightforward enough, isn't it? Can I forgive those men? There's no point in praying the words if I'm prepared to put them into action. God will know if I mean them, even if no one else does. It doesn't look as if I have a lot of options. I've already discovered from painful experience that if I hold a grudge against someone it is me who suffers. I become bitter and full of resentment. My views on forgiveness are already sorted out, and fresh in my mind. There is no real problem in praying for the men. I know the consequences of not forgiving others, and do not intend to be destroyed by them a second time....For once I agree with Dad."

Above all, said Jill, "God has made me new. The pain is still there, but I'm a new person who could really understand. I've never asked Him why it happened to me, I just said, 'OK, now give me the strength to go on.'

"I think that I've grown a lot closer to God and learned to trust more. Just knowing He loves me where I am keeps me going."

"The Rape of the Vicarage Virgin"

For Reflection

And forgive us our sins, as we ourselves forgive everyone indebted to us (Lk. 11:4).

As I have been reflecting on the stories in this book, and the dozens of new stories that friends and parishioners have been sharing with me, I have come to the conclusion that the greater the crime or offense, the greater the need for the victim to forgive.

Annoyance at the rude checkout counter clerk can go on forever; but murder, rape, abuse, abandonment, imprisonment—all seem to drive the victim to find the only way he or she can be free of the offense. This is not to say that the hurt really didn't matter, but rather that it matters very much, and only radical intervention can free or liberate us from that horror. Otherwise, our identity is forever tied to the person or event that hurt us.

The paradox is that only the victim can do the forgiving. In our story, Michael could forgive someone for knocking him unconscious with his own cricket bat. But forgiveness for the rape was Jill's prerogative, and she had to do it on her own time schedule and in her own way.

I am not even sure that friends should bring up the need for forgiveness, not at the beginning, anyway. The appropriate role for friends and community is first to be emotionally and spiritually supportive of the victim, to express outrage and to demand that justice be done.

I just witnessed an example of this in Miami. A Roman Catholic church was vandalized. The local chapter of the National Conference of Christians and Jews expressed horror and sympathy, and called for the apprehension of the vandals, while the pastor of the church led his congregation in prayers asking pardon for the offender.

If you are bearing some great hurt, you might want to pray for the grace to forgive so that you can put that horrible moment behind you. This is not easy to do and I would suggest you seek out your pastor or an appropriate support group. If we define ourselves by who has hurt us or who hates us, we are forever stuck in the moment we were first hurt, and we are bonded to the person who hurt us. As Christians, we are invited in our baptism to identify ourselves with him who loves us and was willing to die on the cross for us.

If a friend who is a victim comes to mind, you might consider how you might work for justice in that friend's behalf or prevent similar crimes from happening.

O God, the author of peace and lover of concord, to know you is eternal life and to serve you is perfect freedom: Defend us, your humble servants, in all assaults of our enemies; that we, surely trusting in your defense, may not fear the power of any adversaries; through the might of Jesus Christ our Lord. —The Book of Common Prayer

"The Rape of the Vicarage Virgin"

Miracle at Medugorje

For more than fifteen years now, I have been part of an early morning coffee klatsch at Atlantic Beach, Florida. Those of us who get together call ourselves the Dawn Patrol. We meet at 8:00 a.m. at the back of a lounge in a local resort hotel. There are about fifty of us who drop in when we can, and attendance averages eight. The presiding officer of the Dawn Patrol is the former mayor of the seaside village. Our morning meetings have been likened to the liars' bench outside country post offices or even, at our more exalted moments, to the gatherings of Jewish elders at the city gate we read of in the Bible.

Jokes are shared, news exchanged, topics discussed. When I make one of my infrequent appearances, there is likely to be a question relating to some biblical or religious issue. For instance, when the Episcopal Diocese of Massachusetts elected a black woman as their suffragan bishop, her qualifications for the post were hashed over at Dawn Patrol meetings for weeks, or so it seemed.

One morning, a local attorney named Jim asked the group, "Have you ever heard of Medugorje in Yugoslavia?" As a matter of fact, I had just been told about Medugorje by a Roman Catholic priest who had been there the month before. Since June of 1981, this mountain hamlet of approximately four hundred families has been reported as the site of daily appearances of the Virgin Mary at 6:45 p.m. to six young local residents who have become known, collectively, as "the visionaries." She has delivered an urgent message to the people of earth to reconcile with God and bring peace to a dangerously troubled world. When Mary's appearances are finally over, she promises to leave a visible sign on the mountainside.

In spite of the difficulty of travel in the region, and the almost total lack of tourist accommodations, over eleven million visitors have made the pilgrimage to Medugorje. Jim told me that he had made the trip with his son-in-law and written up a brief account of his experience. Would I like to read it? Jim's experience had been positive: "I came back a changed man."

Jim's fourteen-page manuscript was charged with excitement, with the experience of a being in a crowd of thousands, of hearing mass in Croatian, and then, individually, saying the rosary in what seemed like fifty different languages at once. That alone was a miracle in itself and well worth the trip. But Jim reported that he and his son-in-law had also observed a strange solar phenomenon in the early evening sky.

"The sun, clear in the cloudless sky, was surrounded by six other identical suns, spaced equally in a circle around it. Then the six suns vanished and the normal sun remained, but it began instantly to pulsate rapidly, then spin in a clockwise direction. Its color changed swiftly from yellow to pink to white to jet black to gold to pink again, surrounded by clouds, very far away, that also changed in color from pink to white to gold. Then the sun seemed to be at the end of a long tunnel that appeared to spiral in upon itself. I asked Louis, 'Do you see what I see? Do you see the sun spinning and pulsating and dancing in the sky?' Louis answered, 'Yes, I see it.' The two of us stood together, alongside hundreds and hundreds of other people, and watched this incredible solar manifestation of the power of God. It

Miracle at Medugorje

is impossible for me to convey in any words that I know the feelings I had watching this celestial display.

"I also remember thinking, 'How will I ever make anyone at home believe this story when I tell it?' Then I remembered, too, that in the famous story of the apparition of the Virgin Mary at Fatima, in Portugal—an apparition witnessed by three children—that during one of the Virgin's appearances there, the sun danced in the sky and a crowd of twenty thousand pilgrims witnessed it. I really didn't believe the Fatima story when I first heard it. Now I do, since I have seen the phenomenon at Medugorje with my own eyes.

"We all watched the miracle on the hillside, for that is what it *had* to be, for approximately fifteen to twenty minutes. Tears were streaming down my face and Louis', too. I thought, momentarily, that what we were seeing might burn the retina of my eyes; but then it seemed unlikely to me that God would allow any harm to come to those who saw the things that were happening in the sky. In fact, there was no damage to my eyes nor, as far as I know, to anyone else's. I didn't even have any disturbing or long-lasting persistence of the vision when the amazing display stopped.

"We all asked each other, after the phenomenon had stopped, if we had all seen the same thing. All of the stories of the people in our group were, in essence, exactly the same."

The phenomenon occurred once more while Jim was at Medugorje. He hasn't been the same since. He is convinced that he witnessed a miracle.

But the miracle in the skies is not the miracle I am telling you about. Almost as a postscript, Jim alluded to "another miracle" that he experienced after a long talk with a priest at Medugorje. He would not write it down but said he would be willing to share it with me when we next met, three days later.

"What was the other miracle?" I asked.

"It was difficult and it was easy," Jim replied.

"For almost forty years," he continued, "I have hated my mother-in-law. That old lady never approved of my marriage to her daughter, she never approved of me, and she has always made sure that I knew it and that my wife knew it, too. She resents the fact that I have an education, that I am a lawyer. She thinks that the only honest labor is done with your hands.

"For all these years, I have nursed my resentment of her until it is both a terrible festering wound and, at the same time, an old friend. That resentment was my constant companion wherever I went. The good priest I met at Medugorje, Father George, gave me a prayer, one that I found both simple and difficult. 'Come, Holy Spirit, and kindle the fire of love within me.' At first, saying it in regard to my mother-in-law was very, very difficult. It was like diving into a pool of icy water. All my senses and instincts drew back, repelled. But it was only difficult the first time. After that, it became easier and easier—and then the burden was gone."

Jim forgave his mother-in-law, and *that* was his miracle at Medugorje.

For Reflection

Jesus said to them, "Prophets are not without honor except in their own country and in their own house." And he did not do many deeds of power there, because of their unbelief (Mt. 13:57-58).

Miracle at Medugorje

There appears to be a relationship between Jesus' ability to perform miracles and the faith of the people around him. Where the faith level was high, great things happened, but where there was little or no faith, as in Nazareth, he could accomplish very few "deeds of power". In contrast to Nazareth, think of Capernaum on the shores of the Sea of Galilee, where many miracles occurred and where people crowded around the house where Jesus was staying, so that the only way a paralyzed man could be brought to Jesus was for his friends to lower him through the roof (Mk. 2:2-5).

I have been in situations where there was such negativity that even the most eloquent orator could not turn things around. On the other hand, I have been in churches and on retreats where there was such an atmosphere of love and trust and acceptance that all kinds of miracles began to happen.

These passages came to mind when I first heard my friend's account of his trip to Medugorje. What a concentration of faith and hope and love there was in that little town in Yugoslavia. No wonder Jim was finally able to let go of his resentment of his mother-in-law. How could you hold onto hatred in a place like that?

Have you been in a community or church that had any of the qualities of Medugorje? It's exciting when it happens. When it does, people find the strength to do and be things that they never thought possible— even the strength to forgive a mother-in-law.

You might want to think about your relationship to your own community or church. Are you truly a part of them or do you think of yourself as a " community of one"? If this is the case, maybe you're making your spiritual life more complicated—and lonely—than it needs to be. Christians are meant to live in community and to draw the strength of the Holy Spirit from that community.

Come Holy Spirit, fill the hearts of Your faithful and kindle in them the fire of your love. Send forth Your Spirit and they shall be created, and you shall renew the face of the earth. —Prayer used in the Cursillo Movement

Grandma's Candy

When Douglas picked the lemon sourball from his grandmother's candy dish, he had no idea that he was doing anything harmful or anything that could conceivably change either his life or his grandmother's life.

Douglas had only recently moved with his mother and sister into his grandparents' home on Robertson Parkway and it was not really a comfortable arrangement. Douglas's parents were being divorced and the move was an economic necessity. The fact that it enabled him to live in the same town, keep his same friends, go to the same school—those advantages never crossed his mind.

For him it meant that his life was out of control and there wasn't anything he could do about it.

His sister Kelly wasn't all that happy about the move, either. For her it not only meant a new telephone number but having to share that number with her grandmother, of all people. Out of long habit, Grandma answered every call on the first or second ring—and then listened to be sure it wasn't for her or a business call for Grandpa. Having your grandmother monitor your calls was a little too much as far as Kelly was concerned.

Not only that, grandchildren and grandparents viewed Alexander Graham Bell's invention from two totally opposing points of view. For the younger generation, it was a major instrument for use in a well-rounded social life. For the elders, it was there for emergencies, for setting up appointments, and for brief messages. This was all before the days of "call waiting" and it was important to "keep the line open."

Douglas, Kelly, and their mother occupied bedrooms on the third floor of the old Victorian house. They also controlled the ground floor with its high-ceilinged parlor and dining room, separated by great sliding rosewood doors. The second floor belonged to the grandparents who had carved out a spacious one-bedroom apartment there for themselves. The entrance way and the halls of the big house were common space.

Part of the problem for Douglas and Kelly lay right there. The phone rang on the first floor, "in the lobby," and on the second floor, in their grandparents' quarters. Douglas and Kelly were not allowed to receive calls on the second floor, so the ring of the phone was inevitably followed by a scramble down two flights of stairs. Douglas had developed *dashing* into an exact science. He could make it to the second floor in three great leaps, hitting the wall by his grandmother's sofa as he made the turn. Second to first was a quiet slide down the banister. Obviously, here was a generation gap that needed tending.

One did not enter the second floor apartment without permission. The formality of a knock and a clearly stated reason for seeking entrance were required. The grandparents had the only functional television set, a state-of-the-art twelve inch, black-and-white model. They also subscribed to the *National Geographic* and to the *Smithsonian* magazines, and always kept the whole Sunday edition of the *New York Times* until it was replaced by a new edition. Permission to read or watch could indeed be requested and was *sometimes* granted; sometimes it was withheld.

It was on one such visit to his grandparents apartment that Douglas spotted the candy bowl placed on the walnut sideboard. Grandma was engrossed in "The Honeymooners" on television. Without thinking, almost by instinct, he picked out a lemon sourball, his favorite flavor, unwrapped it, and popped it into his mouth.

Grandma's head swiveled from Jackie Gleason to her grandson. "You didn't ask permission. You didn't say, 'please'."

Douglas's response was just as fast. He took the sourball out of his mouth, displayed it to his grandmother, and said, "Well, take it back, then!" He left the sticky piece of candy on the sideboard, walked into the hall, and slammed the door behind him. Then he scrambled up to the relative safety of the third floor.

Kelly called out from her room as he passed, "What was all that about?"

"I'll tell you later." The door to Douglas's room closed with a resounding thud.

Then Douglas's mother came to his room. "What happened?"

Douglas told his mother the whole story, adding his editorial comments about his grandmother and living in his grandparents' house.

It was at least two hours later that everyone heard the noise of someone falling in Grandma's bedroom. Her door was locked and so the door had to be forced. She was lying on the floor beside the bed. She was alive, but her breathing was shallow. She moaned and tried to respond to questions. She really wasn't totally aware of what had happened to her, but kept repeating, "That boy...that boy...that boy!"

THE FORGIVENESS BOOK

An ambulance was called. The paramedics were navigating the stairs down to the lobby with the stretcher when Grandpa came home.

Douglas and Kelly stayed in their rooms while the others went to the hospital. Half asleep and half awake, Douglas heard his mother and his grandfather talking in the hall. He heard his grandfather ask, "What about the boy?" He didn't hear his mother's answer. He also heard the words "wait," "pray," and "50-50."

But the odds were really not in Grandma's favor. At seventy-five, and in frail condition, she had a succession of strokes. Her brain was severely damaged. Douglas visited the hospital once. All of the assembled relatives met him with what appeared to be "glued-on" smiles on their faces. He wondered who knew what. Mainly, he stayed in his room. When going up or down the staircase, he stepped lightly—not like the old days.

They brought Grandma's body back to the house. In the old-fashioned way, she was "laid out" in the front parlor. The room was overflowing with flowers. The whole house was filled with the smell of gladioli. The sliding doors between the front parlor and the dining room were closed, and friends and relatives gathered in the back room with casseroles and cheese dip. Coffee was being brewed incessantly, and wine was served from Grandma's crystal decanters.

The wake lasted for three seemingly endless days and nights. The coffin was then taken away, first to the church for the funeral and then for burial in the churchyard. At the funeral, the choir sang, "The strife is o'er, the battle won, Alleluia." To this day, Douglas finds it hard to sing this hymn on Easter without tearing up and remembering.

Grandma's Candy

Douglas's mother tried to minister to him. She explained that his grandmother had been having "cerebral accidents" for quite awhile; that the stress and strain of having them all move in on her probably had been just too much. She also stressed that the lemon sourball incident was also an accident; that under normal circumstances, Grandma would have been angry for a day or two, and then she would have gotten over it. Yes, he had been rude and impolite to his grandmother—but he had not caused her death; the doctor had spoken of the succession of small cerebral accidents and the inevitable "big one." If anyone was to blame for Grandma's death, it was Douglas's mother's fault, she said, for moving in with her parents instead of striking out on her own.

This helped. Some. They hugged and cried. But Douglas still carried a heaviness, a burden, a regret for what had happened. If only he hadn't gone into his grandmother's apartment that night. He had just been bored and at a loss for something to do. If only he hadn't been so rude, so thoughtless. If only Grandma hadn't called out, "That boy!"

Douglas's grandfather took another approach. And at first, Douglas was afraid of him. On the night of his grandmother's death, his grandfather had come home from the hospital and downed half a bottle of whiskey. He had let out a great, hoarse scream, and then collapsed on his bed.

Following the funeral, Grandpa disappeared with his brothers to Florida, but when he came back, he made a point of including Douglas in his activities. Grandpa had been a building contractor in his younger days; now he made his living doing fire appraisals. "Would Douglas come along and help him measure some buildings?" his grandfather asked. To help Douglas, his grandfather asked Douglas to help him.

"Helping" at first meant holding the end of a long measuring tape and writing numbers in a notebook. Douglas soon learned how to calculate square and cubic footage, sketch simple floor plans, take pictures with an old Kodak, estimate loss and calculate rebuilding costs.

In short, the old man was passing along his trade to his grandson. But he was doing much more than that. Much later in his life, Douglas would hear about God's unconditional love and the grace of forgiveness. But the real forgiveness began when his mother and his grandfather, in the midst of their own pain, reached out to a young, impetuous, rude, disrespectful, very human adolescent and enabled him to live.

For Reflection

Or what woman having ten silver coins, if she loses one of them, does not light a lamp, sweep the house, and search carefully until she finds it? When she has found it, she calls together her friends and neighbors, saying, "Rejoice with me, for I have found the coin that I had lost," Just so, I tell you, there is joy in the presence of the angels of God over one sinner who repents (Lk. 15:8-10).

One thing we need to learn about love is that it is a decision, not a feeling. Romance is a feeling, a wonderful glorious feeling, but love is a decision. Nowhere is this more true than in family life.

When the decision was made for Douglas's family to move in with his grandparents, all sorts of feelings were let loose. You might want to take a few minutes to reflect on what each person in the house-

Grandma's Candy

hold was feeling at the time. Have you been in similar situations in your own family?

What loving decisions were made in order to enable the life of this family to go on? What decisions were made that helped the burden of guilt to be lifted from Douglas?

You might want to reflect on some of the experiences of your own family. What loving decisions have been made around difficult situations that enabled you to let go of your guilt? Are there decisions you might make now that would help someone you love?

Almighty God, you alone can bring into order the unruly wills and affections of sinners: Grant your people grace to love what you command and desire what you promise; that, among the swift and varied changes of the world, our hearts may surely there be fixed where true joys are to be found; through Jesus Christ our Lord, who lives and reigns with you and the Holy Spirit, one God, now and for ever. —The Book of Common Prayer

An Unnatural Act

Some thirty miles southwest of Jacksonville there is a major complex of the Florida prison system. It was here in 1978 that network TV cameras recorded the protests over the execution of John Spenkelink. Today, over two hundred inmates wait here on death row. The prison complex now spreads over some one thousand acres on three campuses that have a prison population of more than five thousand people. All of the facilities are overcrowded and the Florida Division of Correctional Institutions is under court order either to provide more space or to release some of the prisoners.

The inmate responsible for the legal action is a twenty-year resident known as Big Mike. He is a brilliant, self-assured, angry, and arrogant man who had the reputation among his fellow inmates of being a militant atheist and a Christian-basher. So imagine the surprise of the prison chaplain's staff when one day Big Mike signed up for a Kairos retreat weekend.

The word *kairos* is a Greek word for time; it is used in the New Testament to denote "the Lord's time," as opposed to *kronos*, which describes earthly or human time. A Kairos Weekend is an ecumenical expression of Cursillo designed especially for prisoners, and staffed jointly by Episcopalians, Roman Catholics, Lutherans, and others.

The Cursillo movement is centered on a lay retreat weekend. It had its origins in the 1930s in the life of the Roman Catholic Church in Spain. The movement came to the United States after World War II and has since jumped ecclesiastical boundaries into the Episcopal, Lutheran, Presbyterian, and Methodist churches. Cursillo is "a short course" in basic Christianity which affects different people in different ways. An outpouring of love and a tremendous sense of community is involved in the experience. There is nothing secret about it, but there are some surprises.

Big Mike told everyone that he had signed up for Kairos because he had lost a bet. He had put his money on the University of Florida 'Gators and they had lost. It was as simple as that. His fans in the prison population didn't need to worry; he hadn't gone soft. He still didn't have any use for God—but he understood that you got to eat a lot of cookies in the course of a Kairos weekend.

The weekend actually started on a Thursday night and was staffed by lay people—men—from outside. They, in turn, were supported by a larger community who prayed for candidates and staff workers by name. The workers were an eclectic group ranging from ex-convicts to professional people. Staff were simply introduced by their Christian names: only the clergy among them are identified by profession. On Mike's particular weekend, there was a circuit court judge waiting on tables at mealtimes. When the judge's identity became known, many of the inmates were deeply moved to learn that a judge was willing to be their servant.

On Saturday morning, Mike got up to speak. He told the staff that he really appreciated everyone coming into the prison and being so friendly and loving, but he added that he still wasn't buying what the weekend was selling! He knew that there wasn't a God; he never would believe there was a God; but he really did appreciate what the staff was doing. "It was very nice," Mike said.

When the judge was identified, Mike made a point of thanking him for coming and added, "God bless you." The judge reflected, "They raise a funny kind of atheist in here."

Later that day a Lutheran pastor gave a short talk on forgiveness. This led to an exercise in which everyone made a list of people who had hurt them and who they wished to forgive. The lists were placed in a bucket and were burned in front of the altar.

The pastor told his own story—how two years before, he had come home to find his wife's body on the floor. She had been raped and murdered. Initially, the pastor himself had been the prime suspect in the crime but the actual rapist was later identified and convicted. He was a man from out of state who had appeared with his family at the pastor's church one Sunday, with no job and no place to live. The pastor and his wife took the strangers into their home to help them get back on their feet. The stranger returned the favor with rape and murder.

The pastor told the Kairos group that he had been able to forgive the man, who was now on death row, because forgiveness was an act of will, not of the emotions. While he still had moments of anger, he continued to renew his act of forgiveness and that God had blessed the act and it was taking over his heart. The pastor added that he was trying to visit the man on death row, but it had not yet been arranged

The talk had a profound effect on staff and candidates alike. Mike was deeply moved by what he had heard but it wasn't until the next day that he told anyone what was happening to him.

"You guys know me and you know I tell it like it is. I've been up all night trying to figure this thing out. I always said I would never believe in God unless I saw a miracle—and I was convinced I never would see one. But last night I *did* see a miracle."

Mike pointed to the pastor.

"There is no way that any human being on earth could forgive someone who did what was done to the pastor and his wife. It is absolutely unnatural to forgive in a situation like that. And something that goes against natural law can only be called supernatural. And if that is true, then there must be a God and I thank God for sending his Son Jesus Christ to be my savior."

Mike added that he was going to write the governor of the state. "What I did in suing the State of Florida for overcrowding was the right thing, but I did it for the wrong reasons. I did it out of hatred and revenge rather than out of love and concern."

"I thought, " he said, "I was coming here for cookies and for good food. I didn't realize that this was the road to Damascus."

For Reflection

But when he came to himself he said, "How many of my father's hired hands have bread enough and to spare, but here I am dying of hunger! I will get up and go to my father, and I will say to him, "Father, I have sinned against heaven and before you; I am no longer worthy to be called your son..." (Lk. 15:17-19).

It has been wisely said that the Parable of the Prodigal Son is the Gospel in miniature. If I had only one page from Scripture with which to convey the essence of Christianity, I would pick this one. Certainly it is at the very core of what this book is all about: asking for forgiveness, granting forgiveness, receiving forgiveness, and reconciliation.

There is not a story in this book that could not be followed by a reflection using the Parable of the Prodigal Son. Why did I choose to use it here?

I chose this parable to go with the story of Big Mike because it has something to say about that moment of truth that is described in Scripture by the phrase, "when he came to himself."

Friends in Alcoholics Anonymous tell me that they were unable to do anything about their drinking until they "hit bottom," which usually means exhausting all of the possibilities that would enable them to continue drinking. They will hasten to add that not everyone has the same "bottom." Sometimes friends and family may intervene and provide that moment of truth where the alcoholic can perceive what his or her drinking is doing to others and to themselves. Some of my AA friends identify very strongly with the prodigal son and that moment when " he came to himself."

I believe that the prodigal son was able to face the stark reality of where his own life had led him because he had the memory or model of another way of life. There was something about his leave-taking from his father that enabled him to come home. His father hadn't slammed the door. There was the memory of how his father treated the people who worked for him—far better than the treatment meted out to the prodigal son by the world at large.

Big Mike's conversion occurred when he found himself in a community where the Gospel was really being lived out: first, with the outside community that had come to the prison to provide music and cookies; then with people like the judge who had come to serve; and then the Lutheran pastor who had found the supernatural power to do something "unnatural."

Mike "came to himself" when he discovered that there was another way to live and a community in which that living could take place.

You may want to read the entire parable of the Prodigal Son. It's found in Luke 15:11-32. In terms of what we have been talking about here, you might want to reflect on your own way of life and where it has gotten you or where you are going with it. Is there another way for you? What about the religious community in which you live? Is it like the elder brother? Would it or could it welcome home the prodigal?

Merciful God, creator of all the peoples of the earth and lover of souls: Have compassion on all who do not know you as you are revealed in your Son Jesus Christ; let your Gospel be preached with grace and power to those who have not heard it; turn the hearts of those who resist it; and bring home to your fold those who have gone astray; that there may be one flock under one shepherd, Jesus Christ our Lord. — The Book of Common Prayer

If You Love Somebody

Conducting chapel services for high school students is no easy task, even when you are the designated chaplain of a church-affiliated school. No matter what the catalogue says about a "Christian school" or "growing within a Christian community," the students are not crazy about chapel services.

As chaplain of the Jacksonville Episcopal High School, it was, nevertheless, my duty to provide a weekly chapel experience that was both meaningful and challenging, inclusive of many religious traditions and points of view, and sensitive to the great diversity within the student body and faculty.

We tried holding chapel services by grade. That meant six services a week. Sometimes we met under the school's great oak tree—an oak, the school catalogue suggested, as old as the Magna Carta. Or we would sit on the river bank, meditate by the pond, or gather in the lecture hall while some bearded alumnus picked at a guitar or read poetry. We even had one younger faculty member prove the mathematical probability of the existence of God on the lecture hall blackboard while half the class and two teachers fell asleep. Chapel services at the Jacksonville Episcopal High School were a distinct challenge.

When all else failed, our standard, bread and butter item was "all-school chapel." With students and faculty and a few visitors and parents, this meant a gathering of over seven hundred people for the Eucharist. The school chorus and even the school band worked on special numbers for these services. Students and faculty would be asked to read lessons and prayers, the art department would do "something creative" on the walls and windows, and all baptized persons were invited to receive Holy Communion.

Another feature of some of the all-school chapels was a guest preacher or speaker. When at all possible, priests or ministers from other denominations were invited to occupy the school pulpit. I have watched some of Jacksonville's leading clergy die a slow death in that pulpit. The students were a very discerning lot who could spot a warmed-over last-Sunday's sermon at fifty paces. Courtesy demanded two minutes of attention from the congregation. After that, the preacher was on his or her own. Oh, nobody booed, hissed, or got up and left. That was poor form and not allowed. But the keen-eared could hear the muffled sound of textbooks being opened and inserted in front of our folder of contemporary Christian songs.

The worst word a speaker at all-school chapel could use was " should." I got to the point that when I invited guest speakers, I would say to them, " Don't say 'should' to the students. If you do, they'll tune you out. And don't use your sermon from last Sunday, no matter how much you think the people at your church liked it. Students *will* listen to an individual tell the story of a personal journey in faith." The speakers who ignored this advice lived to regret it and were never invited back again.

One successful chapel occurred when a scheduled guest speaker canceled and the home team had to go to the plate. The assistant chaplain, Father George, and I flipped a coin to see who would preach. I lost the toss and got the assignment.

The current box office success at the Five Star CINE was *Love Story* with Ryan O'Neal and Ali McGraw. There was a beautiful musical theme in the film that all the top-forty stations were running. There were posters depicting the film's ill-starred young lovers everywhere, and there was no escaping the lone line from the film that everyone quoted: "Love means never having to say you're sorry." I hated that line. It just wasn't true. Imagine trying to have a marriage or a friendship without saying "I'm sorry." But if I wanted to refer to the film and to that line in particular in my sermon—and I was sorely tempted—I needed to avoid saying the fatal "should" to the students and thus fall into the trap of preaching *at* them rather than *to* them.

I found a *Love Story* poster at the local mall and Ted Rickard, the school's music director, bought a copy of the film's omnipresent theme song, which he practiced on his new harpsichord! The next morning the kids ambled into the gymnasium (converted into a chapel) trying to be cool about the whole thing. The school chorus sang some warm-up numbers. We tried an opening hymn: "They will know we are Christians by our love." A Jewish student read the *Shema* in Hebrew and English from Deuteronomy: "Hear, O Israel, the Lord your God is one and you shall love the Lord your God...." The president of the senior class stumbled through 1 Corinthians 13: "Love is patient and kind...." Father George read the gospel from John: "If you love me, you will keep my commandments...." I thought we had established the "love" theme.

Then it was my turn. As I walked to the pulpit, Ted began to play his harpsichord. I stood silent for a good sixty seconds. Chemistry books and French review vocabularies began to be lowered. I unrolled the

If You Love Somebody

poster. The music got bolder. I recited the film's famous line with suitable feeling: "Love means never having to say you're sorry." Then I tore up the poster.

What I had intended as an attention-getter called forth the one and only standing ovation I ever received at the school for one of my sermons. I had planned to say a lot about forgiveness but, thank God, I had the sense just to sit down. It was the shortest sermon I have ever preached. If you love somebody, you *have* to say you're sorry.

For Reflection

And if the same person sins against you seven times a day, and turns back to you seven times and says, "I repent," you must forgive (Lk. 17:4).

The language of relationships and the language of prayer are the same: please, thank you, I'm sorry, I love you, and listen.

When we fail to take, or refuse to take, responsibility for our behavior, our relationships and our prayer life are doomed. How refreshing and healthy it is for one human being to say to another, "It was my fault; I'm sorry; I didn't mean to hurt you."

In the marriage service in the Book of Common Prayer, there is a prayer for the couple that very wisely reinforces this point. "Give them grace, when they hurt each other, to recognize and acknowledge their fault, and to seek each other's forgiveness and yours."

Take a few minutes to think of any relationships that would be strengthened by a simple apology or request for forgiveness.

Then take a few minutes to reflect on any aspect of your relationship to God that could be strengthened by an act of penitence.

Make their life together a sign of Christ's love to this sinful and broken world, that unity may overcome estrangement, forgiveness heal guilt, and joy conquer despair. —The Book of Common Prayer

Over His Dead Body

From all outward appearances, Al Thompson had everything. He was married to a beautiful woman, Sally, and they had two fine young sons. Al had a good job and a four-bedroom, two-and-a-half-bathroom house in the suburbs—with a swimming pool! The Thompsons' attendance at church was more than perfunctory. They appeared to have a deep faith, said prayers with the children at meals and at bedtime, read the Bible, and tithed. Al was a joy to have on the vestry. He had a light touch with people and a generally positive attitude.

Al was caught off balance one day by a totally unexpected phone call, one that brought back a rush of memories and feelings he thought he had buried. He was surprised by the call and even more surprised by his own reaction to it. A great rush of bitterness and anger overcame him when a nurse from a hospital called to say that his father was dead.

Al had not heard from his father in years, didn't know that he was still alive until that day, and didn't care that he was dead. His father had abandoned his family when Al was eight, leaving memories of alcoholic vomit, beatings, and a childhood lived in near poverty.

"We need to have you come by and sign some papers," the voice on the other end said.

"Why is that?" Al heard himself say.

"You're listed as next of kin. He's your father, we need...."

"He's never been a father to me."

"We have to have your signature so that we can dispose of the body."

"I don't care what you do with it. It can stay there and rot for all I care."

"But Mr. Thompson," the nurse pleaded. That's all she got to say. Al banged the receiver down, stood up, brushed by his wife and children, and walked out into the night.

His wife, Sally, called me the next day and told me what had happened. "Maybe you can get to him," Sally said. "He won't say a word to me."

Al didn't say anything to me either; at least not for awhile. To all outward appearances, he was his usual cool, cheerful self. When I expressed my sympathy, he cut me short with "Thank you for your concern."

Some twelve months later, Al went on a retreat weekend, and when he returned, I could tell that something had changed. Before I could ask him, he invited me to breakfast.

"You know about my dad?" he said over a cup of coffee.

"All that I know is that he died."

Al told me of the phone conversation with the nurse at the hospital, and of the almost blind rage that had overcome him. He did not go to the hospital or the funeral home, but he did go to the cemetery the day after the burial.

"I waited until it was almost dark and they were about to lock the gates. I found the grave, stood over it, unzipped my trousers, and urinated all over it. I don't know whether I spilled more piss or tears on the ground.

"But that's not what I wanted to tell you," Al added. "The story has a happy ending. You know, I went on that retreat. They had a lot to say about forgiveness, both receiving it and giving it. When the

Over His Dead Body

weekend was over, they gave each one of us a cross. The retreat leader said something that really got to me. He said that if I had been the only person in the world and the worst sinner, the Lord still would have died on the cross for me."

Al took a deep breath. "On my way home from the retreat, I went back to the cemetery where my father is buried, dug a hole, and put the cross in his grave.

"I wet the ground again, but this time there were only tears, tears of joy. At last I was free."

For Reflection

For you did not receive a spirit of slavery to fall back into fear, but you have received a spirit of adoption. When we cry, "Abba! Father!" it is that very Spirit bearing witness with our spirit that we are children of God (Rom. 8:15-16).

Shortly after Al had told me his story, he was able to share it with a group of men from the parish. Not knowing how his revelation would be received, he was quite nervous, but the risk he took paid off not only for him, but for everyone else. Almost every man there expressed some deep disappointment in his relationship with his father.

In some cases the father was absent all or most of the time; in others he was either too lenient or too demanding. The list was endless, but its common thread was the rift between parent and child. The men decided that not only would they try to do a better job with their own children, but they also needed to forgive their fathers. They also knew there was only one perfect parent, who was available to all of them.

This might be a good time to reflect on our relationships to our parents, remembering that they are frail, vulnerable human beings just like us...perhaps a little too much like us for our own comfort. Give thanks for the good things they did, forgive them for their shortcomings and failures, and turn to the one perfect parent who is available to us at any time of the day or night.

O God our Father, please make up the difference between the love we needed and the love we received.
—Prayer attributed to the late Ruth Carter Stapleton

Will Someone Go With Me?

My wife Lynne loves oysters. She has been known to disappear for hours at an oyster roast, only to be discovered gorging herself on the ugly contents of those distorted, wart-covered shells. Once, at an Oktoberfest advertising "as many oysters as you can eat," she was seated next to a courtly old family doctor. She had been eyeing the oyster bar and, seeing a vacant space or two, could control herself no longer.

"I feel an attack coming on," she announced, her way of excusing herself from the table.

The doctor, not being privy to Lynne's coded message, asked, "Do you have these attacks very often?"

"At least once or twice a year," my spouse replied.

Bringing his best "bedside manner" into play, the doctor continued to probe, "How long do these attacks last?"

"At least an hour. Sometimes two hours," stated Lynne, completely oblivious to the misunderstanding building between them.

I rescued Lynne just as the doctor began to reach for her pulse. She marched off to the oyster bar. I did not envy her. (My nomination for the world's bravest person is the individual who first ate an oyster.) I had grown up near the water and, as a little kid, I had dug for clams and oysters with my grandfather. While I loved Grandpa, it really turned my stomach when he pulled a clam or oyster out of the mud, swished it clean in a tidal pool, opened it with his knife, and ate the contents of the shell—raw.

But whenever I think of oysters, I think of Bill and Connie Sharkey. Bill is a semi-retired Episcopal priest who lives in the best of all possible worlds. He and Connie live in Cedar Key, on Florida's West Coast. Cedar Key is one of our state's few remaining undiscovered and unspoiled fishing villages. Bill draws his pension and social security, and conducts services and provides pastoral care for the congregation of Christ Church, overlooking the Gulf of Mexico.

Lynne and I worked out a weekend exchange with the Sharkeys. They would stay in our rectory in Orange Park, while Bill took services at Good Samaritan. I would do the Sunday duty at Christ Church, and Lynne and I would both enjoy a weekend on the Gulf of Mexico.

We had always thought of the Sharkeys as a happy-go-lucky couple who exuded joy and didn't have a care in the world. The first part was true, but our second supposition was seriously off, as we were to learn over that weekend. But first there was the encounter with the oysters.

We arrived at Cedar Key in time for dinner on Thursday evening. Connie and Bill were busy in the kitchen working over a freshly harvested burlap sack of oysters. "The first course is going to be oysters on the half shell," Connie announced. Lynne grinned. I winced.

Bill invited me outside to look over his motor boat and Lynne stayed in the kitchen with Connie. "Please find a way to tell Connie I can't eat raw oysters," I whispered to Lynne as I went out the door.

When we were all seated at the dinner table, Connie announced, "Lynne tells me you don't eat raw oysters so I've made you a bowl of oyster stew."

I winced again, inwardly, and Lynne gave me a sympathetic grin. Obviously, I was on my own. Now,

Connie's oyster stew wasn't the ordinary watery concoction resembling potato soup with a fishy taste that you get at good old Captain Fishbait's. Oh no. There were twelve oysters in the bowl before me about the size of golf balls. I knew I would offend our host and hostess deeply if I declined to eat it. I also knew I would throw up if I ever tried to chew one of those little wads of aquatic protoplasm. Only one course of action was open: swallow them whole; gulp them down. Lynne had averted her eyes; she obviously didn't want to watch. My only consolation was the thought that maybe it was true that oysters were an aphrodisiac.

Meanwhile, the table conversation had turned to children. Bill and Connie spoke of having five children, but only three appeared—as grownups—in the photographs on their wall. It seems that their first child, Sally Robbins Sharkey, had been born June 29, 1947, with multiple birth defects. She was baptized four days later and died shortly after that; her body was given for research. Sally's ministry to her parents proved to be profound. She set the young couple on a pilgrimage of faith that was to lead Bill into the Episcopal priesthood.

Sally's birth and death had been followed by the arrival, in fairly rapid succession, of four healthy children: two boys and two girls. Griff, a boy, was the youngest of them all.

By 1960 Bill had completed his theological training, was ordained, and was assigned to his first cure as vicar of Christ Church, Tracy City, Tennessee. It was a mountain mission congregation, not too far from Bill's seminary at the University of the South in Sewanee, Tennessee. The ministry flourished. The Sharkeys were as happy as—two oysters at high tide.

In the winter of 1963, disaster struck. Connie told the story. "The first snowfall of the year was a good one. We had given Griff a sled for Christmas and he was very eager to try it out for the first time. As he donned his snow gear and headed for the door, he asked the rest of the family, his sisters and brother, his daddy, and me, if we wanted to go sledding with him. No one would—each one of us had something that seemed more pressing at the time. As our nine-year-old went out the door, his voice echoed, 'I wish someone would go with me.'"

Connie remembers that she was taking a nap later in the day when she heard the knock on the door. Griff had been in an accident, hit by a car. An ambulance had been called.

As they tried to reconstruct what had happened, it emerged that Griff was on his way home from sledding with his friends in a restricted, roped-off area. Connie speculates that "the hill down towards our street was just too inviting for a nine-year-old to pass up. The only problem was that at the bottom of the hill there were stone walls making it impossible to see into the street from either side. The snow had melted and refrozen. It had become solid ice. An old man drove his car around the corner. It was impossible for him to stop."

The old man's one recollection was that he had seen Griff "coming down the hill, lickety split, with a grin from ear to ear. He was having a ball!"

This fact was a comfort to Bill and Connie. "It meant so much to know that he was having a good time and was evidently not aware of or frightened by the oncoming disaster. He never knew what hit him and probably never saw the car."

Initially, the local doctor diagnosed a concussion and a broken leg. The ambulance was sent on to the hospital in Chattanooga. The Bishop of Tennessee met the Sharkeys at the hospital. Griff never regained consciousness. He died that night.

There was a great outpouring of love and concern from old friends and parishioners. Food arrived for weeks. People shared words of comfort or just gave family members a hug when they met them. Their faith had carried the Sharkeys along with their certainty that Griff was with God. Connie was to write later, "The gift of God is eternal life. Griff knew God and believed—so I know where he is."

Connie remembers ironing Griff's Cub Scout uniform. His body lay in state in the church. Parishioners kept a vigil night and day. So did Griff's dog Curly who sat on the front steps of the church until the boy's body was taken to the cemetery.

Three months later a friend called Connie and asked how she was doing.

"I hesitated for a moment and then said, in all honesty, that the cookie had crumbled! The terrible guilt I felt for the fact that I had not gone with Griff on that winter day surfaced. It was awful. I was tormented."

Connie had to face the fact that she had been avoiding the issue of the circumstances of Griff's death, and she did so in the only way she knew how—with prayer and the listening ear of a Christian friend. Over the course of several days, she poured out her feelings. "I told the Lord all about it and he, in his mercy, gave me his forgiveness, completely, absolutely. Forgiveness is glorious!"

Connie felt like a new creature, as if the chains binding her had been broken. She began to tell her story to others when it seemed right; she went on a retreat at a nearby conference center and told her story to those who would listen. Then she began to wonder if she was talking too much. She prayed about this, too, and she relates, " The Lord said in no uncertain terms, 'this is not yours to cherish; it is yours to share.'"

We were now well into the night, and I realized I had forgotten all about the oysters.

For Reflection

Come to me, all you that are weary and are carrying heavy burdens, and I will give you rest (Mt. 11:28).

When I was in school, it was popular to parody Sigmund Freud's teachings by saying, "Anybody who feels guilty ought to be ashamed of himself!"

Then along came Dr. Karl Menninger, the great American psychiatrist, who argued in his last book, *Whatever Became of Sin?*, that guilt was indeed an appropriate human response if you had, in fact, done something bad. The old name for such bad behavior was *sin*, and the cure was repentance and forgiveness.

But what about the parents in this story, Connie and Bill? No one judged them guilty, but Connie *felt* guilty. If only she had gone out with her son. No one held her responsible for his death, but she *felt* responsible.

Connie was weighed down with a " heavy burden" and she placed it quietly at the altar, where she had learned over the years to bring lesser concerns. It is interesting to note that here was no moment of conversion, no peal of thunder or voice from heaven. All she knew was that she had been in pain and the pain was now gone. She had felt guilty and now she felt forgiven.

Will Someone Go With Me?

There is an old spiritual that chants, "I'm gonna lay my burden down," words that hold a lot of truth. Reflect for a while on the events in your life that still carry a sting. Is there something you can do about them? Might the words, "Come to me" be an answer?

Set us free, O God, from the bondage of our sins, and give us the liberty of that abundant life which you have made known to us in your Son our Savior Jesus Christ; who lives and reigns with you, in the unity of the Holy Spirit, one God, now and for ever.
—The Book of Common Prayer

The Man in the County Jail

It was one of the more celebrated murders—make that homicides—of the year. A civic leader, well know in his community, married to the daughter of a prominent family, had strangled his wife to death.

It was all over the front page of the morning paper. The crime had occurred in the early afternoon when the accused had returned home unexpectedly. The accused had phoned the police within minutes of his wife's death. Attempts at resuscitation failed. The victim was pronounced DOA at the local hospital. The accused was in the county jail. When the children returned from school, they were taken into temporary custody by the juvenile authorities. The victim's parents were flying in from London, where they had been located at the first stop on a European holiday tour.

I drank my second cup of coffee and turned to the editorial page. The phone rang. It was the senior warden of a neighboring parish. Their rector was out of town and couldn't be reached. He had left word that in case of emergency, I should be called. Had I read the morning paper?

"As far as the editorial page," I replied.

"Did you see the headlines about Ben and Sylvia Smith? [The names have been changed.] They're members here, you know."

"Yes, I saw; and, no, I didn't know."

The senior warden filled me in on the details, known facts, and neighborhood gossip. Would I go with him to the jail to see Ben?

A county jail is a cold and matter-of-fact place. There is a routine and a procedure for everything. Yes, I could see the prisoner. The senior warden could not. I took my turn being processed. I signed in. They checked me over. Metal clanged against metal. Doors opened and shut. Keys turned. Knuckles clutched thick bars. Lonely eyes searched the corridors for a familiar face.

I came to Ben's cell. He did not know me—but my clerical collar established an immediate relationship. He was filled with grief and remorse for Sylvia.

He expressed the desire to attend her funeral. This request was denied by the sheriff, and violently and understandably opposed by Sylvia's father, who had also decreed that the service would be conducted by a minister of his denomination, not her husband's.

I offered to be with Ben at the time of Sylvia's funeral and conduct a memorial eucharist. He wanted this very much.

I returned on the appointed day and hour. The guard checked me over and examined my communion kit with great curiosity, grunting as he handled the miniature chalice, paten, and cross. I still don't know whether he was looking for contraband or if it was simply that he had never seen these items before.

We improvised an altar on the edge of the bed.

This took place before the new Book of Common Prayer was issued. They say that the old 1928 Prayer Book was penitential in nature, but for this occasion, it couldn't have been more appropriate.

"We acknowledge and bewail our manifold sins and wickedness....

"The remembrance of them is grievous unto us; the burden of them is intolerable. Have mercy....

" For thy Son our Lord Jesus Christ's sake, forgive us all that is past....

" This is a true saying, and worthy of all men to be received, that Christ Jesus came into the world to save sinners....

" If any man sin, we have an Advocate with the Father, Jesus Christ the righteous; and he is the propitiation for our sins....

" We are not worthy so much as to gather up the crumbs under thy table...that our sinful bodies may be made clean by his body, and our souls washed through his most precious blood..."

When Ben lifted his hands to receive communion, I hesitated for a moment.

Those hands were the murder weapons. It takes a fraction of a second to pull a trigger or plunge a knife, but it had taken three to five minutes of sustained anger pressing those hands against Sylvia's throat to remove her life. Now those same hands were reaching out.

How the Gospel of Jesus Christ became real at that moment!

" Our sinful bodies made clean by his body. Our souls washed through his most precious blood."

For Reflection
For my iniquities overwhelm me;
like a heavy burden they are too much for me to bear.
My heart is pounding, my strength has failed me,
and the brightness of my eyes is gone from me.
My friends and companions draw back
from my affliction;
my neighbors stand afar off (Ps. 38:4, 10, 11).

I can remember as a young acolyte watching the priest pound his chest just before taking communion

The Man in the County Jail

and saying, "I am not worthy, I am not worthy." It wasn't in the prayer book, but I was assured that it was an ancient and apostolic tradition. The message it conveyed was that no one was "worthy" to receive Holy Communion. No one was good enough—not the bishop, not the parish priest—to earn the right to be admitted to the Lord's Table.

Admission to the Holy Communion was based on another set of criteria: "Ye who do truly and earnestly repent you of your sins, and are in love and charity with your neighbors, and intend to lead a new life, following the commandments of God, and walking from henceforth in his holy ways; Draw near with faith, and take this holy Sacrament to your comfort, and make your humble confession to Almighty God, devoutly kneeling."

There is something here that lies at the very heart of the Gospel. No one is worthy to have the Lord come under their roof. No one is so good that they have earned the right to receive the Eucharist. Nor is anyone so bad that they cannot be touched and redeemed by God's love.

When you reflect on the dramatic contrast the priest in the story experienced between the communion bread and the murderer's hands, you might ask yourself if there is any part of your life you are withholding from Christ's touch.

We do not presume to come to this thy Table, O merciful Lord, trusting in our own righteousness, but in thy manifold and great mercies. We are not worthy so much as to gather up the crumbs under thy Table. But thou art the same Lord whose property is always to have mercy. Grant us therefore, gracious Lord, so to eat the flesh of thy dear Son Jesus Christ, and to drink his blood, that we may evermore dwell in him, and he in us. —The Book of Common Prayer

The Man in the County Jail

Father Forgive

It was Sunday morning in the summer of 1968. Jim Long and I had boarded a train at Paddington Station, headed for Coventry. Jim was press officer for the Episcopal Church; he and I were on the "International Communication Team" in London, covering the Lambeth Conference of Anglican bishops from around the world. Lambeth happens every ten years and the bishops gather at the invitation of the Archbishop of Canterbury.

As the train made its way through the London suburbs, we both noticed a red-haired young cleric wearing a bright purple vest standing at the other end of the coach. "He looks awfully young to be a bishop," Jim said. "I wonder if he's one of ours?"

"Let's find out," I said as I started to maneuver the aisle to the other end of the car.

The youthful bishop, still in his thirties, it turned out, was Edmond L. "Red" Browning, newly consecrated Bishop of Okinawa. Ed, who had been trained as a missionary, was fluent in Japanese and, prior to his election as bishop, had been archdeacon of Okinawa, coordinating the missionary efforts of both English-and Japanese-speaking congregations. He was, in a very real sense, one of the last missionary bishops of the Episcopal Church. In 1971 when Okinawa was returned, politically speaking, to Japan, Browning resigned so that the Diocese of Okinawa could more comfortably come under the jurisdiction of the Japanese Episcopal Church—the Nippon Seikokai.

Ed was by himself. He, too, was heading for Coventry Cathedral and he welcomed the invitation to join us.

The road from Coventry's British Rail station led us to a large open area in front of the ancient city's new cathedral. We came upon it rather suddenly, and the magnificence of it was startling—the old gothic tower in the distance with the graceful new stone and glass structure in the foreground, and a pedestrian walkway cutting through the center.

On the facade of the new cathedral, in double life size, were the bronze figures of the Archangel St. Michael, wings unfurled, standing over a prostrate and defeated figure of the devil. The sculpture was the last work completed, before his death, of Britain's great contemporary sculptor, Sir Jacob Epstein. In the eternal battle between good and evil, St. Michael was about to thrust his spear into the chest of humanity's eternal adversary.

We stopped to take in the sight. And as we stood there, we overheard two English ladies, visitors like us, discussing the sculpture.

"He's kind of handsome, isn't he?" one woman said to the other.

"Who, St. Michael?"

"No," she said with a bit of a cackle, "the devil!"

We entered the new cathedral and spent most of the day admiring Graham Sutherland's great tapestry, visiting the baptistry, with its magnificent contemporary stained glass designed by John Piper and fashioned by Patrick Reyntiens, and meditating in the Gethsemane Chapel, with its golden mosaic by Steven Sykes. But the most lasting impression came when we entered the ruins of Coventry's fourteenth-century cathedral, destroyed by Germany's Luftwaffe bombers on the night of November 14, 1940, during the Battle of Britain. Only the tower, the shell of the outer walls, and the high altar remain.

Part of Coventry's continuing tradition is the story that on the morning following the raid, the cathedral clergy, digging in the rubble, fashioned one cross of burned timbers and a second one of large, iron nails. On the wall behind the altar, they wrote with a piece of charred wood the words, " Father forgive."

The three of us were deeply moved. Ed expressed his strong feelings about the senselessness and cruelty of war. In his ministry in Okinawa, he came in daily contact with the U.S. military personnel going to and from Vietnam. More often than not, he saw the wounded and dead on their way home. So it did not surprise me when, over twenty years later, early in 1991, I heard of Presiding Bishop Edmond L. Browning's opposition to the Persian Gulf War and his personal expression of that point of view to fellow Episcopalians George Bush and James Baker. He told them that the Middle East could be destroyed past the point of recovery, and pleaded with Bush to find a peaceful solution.

Bush responded that he hated " to have his bishop in opposition." Browning replied, " Mr. President, I really do love you and want you to know that I am praying for you every day."

At a meeting two weeks into the Gulf War, Browning told a story to illustrate his point of view about all armed conflict. " I was in Japan for the centennial celebration of the Nippon Seikokai and was asked to lead a peace pilgrimage to Hiroshima. If you have been to the Peace Museum in Hiroshima, you know what a powerful tale it tells of the sorrows and horrors of war. I'm not sure I'm a pacifist, but visiting the Hiroshima museum has come as close as anything to making me one. The first time I visited the Peace Museum, I had a conversion experience.

"One of the people we met in Hiroshima was Tazu Shibama, an eighty-one-year-old survivor of the blast. Shibama was a tiny lady, badly stooped, who looked every bit her age. She told us of her experience on that fateful day when the bomb fell. Hers was a graphic and moving story spoken, if you can believe it, in a soft Tennessee accent, because she had gone to a Methodist school in Nashville. Shibama believed she was spared because God wanted to use her as a witness for peace. And then she said to me: 'I ask your forgiveness for December 7.'"

Bishop Browning reflected that "he was shocked, speechless, moved to a sense of shame and deep repentance that this dear little woman, who had suffered so horribly, would ask for our forgiveness."

When I read those words of my old friend Ed Browning, my mind went back to that summer afternoon at Coventry Cathedral, the cross of nails, and the words written with a charred piece of wood, "Father forgive."

For Reflection

But you will receive power when the Holy Spirit has come upon you; and you will be my witnesses in Jerusalem, in all Judea and Samaria, and to the ends of the earth (Acts 1:8).

As much as I often want to tell someone that what they need to do is forgive, I know that isn't the way to go about it. There are some things people have to do for themselves, and there are certain conclusions they need to arrive at for themselves. The best we can do is to be witnesses to the experiences we ourselves have had of forgiveness.

When I think of my visits to England, I think of the many monuments that cover the landscape, commemorating some act of heroism, some military victory. The same observation might be made on a visit to Washington, D.C. But Coventry Cathedral is the only place that I know where there is a monument to forgiveness. What a strong witness that cross of nails must have been on the morning after the Blitz. What a strong witness that cross of nails has been to those who have visited the new cathedral at Coventry or attended one of its many programs dedicated to world peace, reconciliation, and international understanding.

You might want to think of the models of forgiveness and reconciliation that have influenced your own life. You may want to reflect on the experiences of forgiveness in your own life. Is there someone you know who would be encouraged by hearing your witness?

Eternal God, in whose perfect kingdom no sword is drawn but the sword of righteousness, no strength known but the strength of love: So mightily spread abroad your Spirit, that all peoples may be gathered under the banner of the Prince of Peace, as children of one Father; to whom be dominion and glory, now and for ever. —The Book of Common Prayer

Conclusion

Forgiveness and the Cross

For many years, I participated in an ecumenical television program that included a rabbi, a Roman Catholic priest, the president of a traditionally black college, and a Southern Baptist minister. We learned to discuss, debate, and even disagree, and, for the most part, without losing our tempers. In fact, we became fast friends and looked forward to our recording sessions. One day when we were discussing the Jewish High Holy Days, the rabbi told us about the Jewish tradition of the two seats for God on the Ark of the Covenant that was kept in the Temple. One is the Judgment Seat; the other, the Mercy Seat. "On the Day of Atonement," the rabbi explained, "we believe that God moves from the Judgment Seat to the Mercy Seat."

The eyes of the monsignor lit up. "That's exactly what Christians believe God was doing in Christ upon the cross."

It is important to the theme of this book that the grace we receive to forgive and be forgiven is somehow linked to Jesus Christ's reconciling death for us upon the cross. That Christ died for our sins is something we all learned early in our Sunday school careers. But just what it was that Jesus did on the cross and why he had to do it is something few Christians understand and most of them are willing to accept on faith, leaving it to the theologians to explain.

What we are talking about is redemption and atonement. The word "atonement" really means "at-one-ment," bringing back together and reconciling what has been separated. Earlier in this book, we considered the fact that sin is really separation—separation from God, neighbor, and self. The work of reconciliation is to bring us back into proper relationship with God, neighbor, and self.

Jews observed the Day of Atonement long before the time of Jesus, and in the story with which this book begins, I mentioned the scapegoat, or *azazel*, which had its origins deep within the ancient Semitic tradition. Each year, an animal was chosen to carry the sins and hostilities of the community into the wilderness. Christians add to this the mysterious and poignant passages in Isaiah that refer to the Suffering Servant, which express the voluntary acceptance of a punishment deserved or "earned" by another: "Surely he has borne our griefs and carried our sorrows; yet we esteemed him stricken, smitten by God, and afflicted. But he was wounded for our transgressions, he was bruised for our iniquities; upon him was the chastisement that made us whole, and with his stripes we are healed" (Is. 53:4-5). Christians were quick to see Jesus as that figure who "was numbered with the transgressors, yet bore the sin of many" (Is. 53:12; Mk. 15:28; Lk. 22:37), while Paul was comfortable writing to the Christians in Rome of him "whom God put forward as an expiation by his blood" (Rom. 3:25).

The New Testament has a number of images to describe Christ's work on the cross: it is seen as ransom, penal substitution, priestly sacrifice, vicarious suffering, moral example, victory over Satan, to name only a few. All of these scriptural images point to, yet none completely define, the mystery of

Christ's death on the cross by which we are reconciled to God. Once we are aware of it, we find that everyday life is full of stories and happenings that also shed light on the mystery of the cross and forgiveness in contemporary images and pictures. I would like to conclude with some stories that have come my way which do just that.

I once knew a priest who was called to be a witness in a domestic relations case. He had counseled the couple who were now, it turned out, being divorced, and he was being asked to testify to information revealed in his counseling sessions. The priest refused on the grounds that such sessions were privileged and came under the traditional " seal of the confessional." He quoted The Book of Common Prayer: " The secrecy of a confession is morally absolute for the confessor, and must under no circumstances be broken."

Unfortunately, he was citing church law and not state law, although some states do protect clergy in such situations. The judge found him in contempt of court and fined him a hundred dollars. Then the judge chose to do an unusual thing; he declared the court in recess for fifteen minutes and went out and paid the hundred dollar fine himself. Thus, justice was served.

" There was no other good enough to pay the price of sin."

Another story.

A psychiatrist was attempting to treat a deeply disturbed boy. They met in a room equipped with children's books and toys. The doctor sat cross-legged on the floor, made up games, drew pictures, sang songs, and pointed out the merits of the books. The boy remained withdrawn and unresponsive. Then suddenly, as if activated by some electrical impulse, he grabbed a chair and with rage written all over his face, charged at the doctor with it. The doctor's first impulse was to fend off his assailant with his arms. But instead he took a risk and opened his hands to receive the boy. At the very last minute, the chair fell on the floor and the boy fell into the waiting arms. His recovery had begun.

The world asked Jesus, "How much do you love me?" Jesus threw open his arms and said, "This much." Then they drove in the nails.

On January 13, 1982, Air Florida Flight 90 took off in a blizzard from National Airport in Washington, D.C., and crashed into the Fourteenth Street Bridge. As rescuers fought against the cold and the darkness to recover the few survivors from the icy waters of the Potomac, a heroic drama was being played out. Twice a balding, middle-aged man had a chance to save himself. Twice he took hold of the life line thrown out by rescuers and twice he handed it on to another survivor. When all the other survivors had been saved and it was finally the man's turn, the rescue helicopter hovering over the now sinking tail section of the plane, discovered that the familiar balding head had disappeared beneath the water. Rescue pilot Donald Usher wept when he reported, "He could have gone on the first trip, but he put everyone else ahead of himself." The man was later identified as Arland Williams, a forty-six-year-old divorced bank examiner from Atlanta.

As Christians point to the work of Christ on the cross, they understand that he died that others might have life.

A similar story comes from the annals of the Holocaust. In Ravensbruch, one of the many death camps in Poland, the daily quota of prisoners were being lined up for their walk to the "showers." A Jewish woman, knowing that they were heading to the gas chambers, became, understandably, hysterical with fear. The guards were about to force her along, when a Russian nun, Mother Maria, came forward. "It's all right," she said to the frightened woman, "I'll take your place." It was Good Friday.

Terry Waite, special aide to Robert Runcie, the former Archbishop of Canterbury, began to appear in the secular press in the mid-1980s. He had a special talent for negotiating the release of hostages being held in Middle Eastern countries. Then, in 1987, Waite failed to return to his hotel in Beirut and was held hostage for almost five years until his release. The chapel bell at Lambeth rang daily while the archbishop's staff continued to pray for the release of their colleague. In a very real sense, Terry Waite had become a "ransom for many." He knew the risk he was taking and he left strict instructions that a ransom must not be paid for his release.

In Ruell Howe's book *Man's Need and God's Action*, there is the account of a mother-daughter confrontation. When the daughter determined she wasn't going to get her own way, she stormed up the stairs. But instead of going to her own room, she slipped into her mother's sewing room. There, hanging on the door, was an evening dress that had just been completed. In her anger, the girl took a pair of scissors and hacked wildly at the dress. Her mother came in and, seeing the devastation lying all around, collapsed, near hysterics, on the bed.

There was a long space of silence. Finally, the daughter spoke: "Mother, please!"

And she continued to repeat those two words, seemingly endlessly—"Mother, please!"

Finally the mother lifted her head. "Mother, please—what?"

Forgiveness and the Cross

"Mother please take me back."

Mother and daughter, in tears, embraced.

During the course of a Cursillo retreat weekend, I heard this story told as part of a reflection on Christ's work on the cross. At the intersection of a busy waterway and the mainline of a railroad, there was a drawbridge. It stayed open except when a train was coming through. One day, the bridge tender brought his son, a young boy, to work with him. They had a splendid time watching the boats sail through, and lowering and raising the bridge when a train arrived. It was mid-afternoon when the tender heard the whistle of an express passenger train; the usual early warning signal had failed to go off. The train was less than a minute away.

The man looked for his son—he wasn't in the tender's booth. The father looked out the window at the drawbridge below. Somehow, his son had slipped out the door and was playing among the massive gears of the bridge machinery. He called out to the boy but the son didn't hear his father's voice. A decision had to be made. Either the tender rescued his son and forfeited the lives of the hundreds of people aboard the train who would plunge through the open drawbridge into the water below, or he could lower the bridge.

The tender's hand grabbed the control lever. He closed the bridge. The express train came through. The passengers were saved. His son was lost.

Christians see a parallel between Abraham's sacrifice of Isaac (Gen. 22:1-19) and the sacrifice of Christ on the cross. When Abraham and his son were walking up the mountain with wood for a burnt offering, Isaac became suspicious. He wanted to know where the sacrificial animal was, and his father replied, "God himself will provide the lamb..." To reconcile the division between God and the human race, which was resolved once and for all time on the cross, God himself provided the lamb.

O Lamb of God, that takest away the sins of the world, have mercy upon us.
O Lamb of God, that takest away the sins of the world, have mercy upon us.
O Lamb of God, that takest away the sins of the world, grant us thy peace.

Biblical Resources

Joseph and His Brothers
Genesis 37;39-47

The story of Joseph is one of the most highly detailed biographical accounts in the Hebrew Bible. For our purposes, it provides an excellent study of many of the issues of family life, including alienation and reconciliation. From Chapter 44 on, we have a touching description of grace at work in bringing a family back together. Joseph's resentment is mitigated by the realization that God has used a set of bad circumstances to bring about good things.

The Suffering Servant
Isaiah 53

This is the best known of the "servant" passages in Isaiah and is a vital link between the Hebrew Bible and the Christian Scriptures. It is a key to understanding the atoning work of Christ. "He bore the sin of many, and made intercession for the transgressors."

David and Bathsheba
2 Samuel 11:1—12:25

This episode in the life of King David has all of the excitement and intrigue of a political exposé in a modern tabloid newspaper. Religion, sex, and power are the magic ingredients; but there is also a twist. When confronted with his crime, King David confesses and seeks forgiveness.

Penitential Psalms
Psalms 6, 22, 25, 32, 38, 40, 51, and 130

Psalm 51, "Wash me through and through from my
wickedness and cleanse me from my sin," is generally acknowledged as *the* penitential psalm. It is used
by Christians on Ash Wednesday and by Jews on the
Day of Atonement. It is often associated with King
David's confession (2 Sam. 12:13).

Leave Your Gift
Matthew 5:21-26
The importance of reconciliation to the Christian
life is highlighted by Jesus in the Sermon on the
Mount. "Leave your gift there before the altar and
go; first be reconciled to your brother or sister."

The Lord's Prayer
Matthew 6:9-15
Also part of the Sermon on the Mount, Jesus not
only gives his followers a prayer including petitions
for forgiveness, but adds a commentary linking forgiving and forgiveness. "If you do not forgive others,
neither will your Father forgive your trespasses."

If Your Brother Sins Against You
Matthew 18:15-20
Jesus emphasizes the need for reconciliation,
especially among members of the church. He out-
lines a process to enable reconciliation to happen.

Seventy Times Seven
Matthew 18:21-35
Jesus answers the question posed by Peter, "How
often should I forgive?" Just to make sure everyone
gets the point, he adds a parable about an unforgiv-
ing servant.

The Woman Who Was a Sinner
Luke 7:36-50

This unplanned encounter at a dinner party with a woman of uncertain virtue becomes the occasion for Jesus to teach a basic truth. "Her sins, which were many, have been forgiven; hence she has shown great love. But the one to whom little is forgiven, loves little."

The Prodigal Son, the Loving Father, the Resentful Brother
Luke 15:11-32

This is the classic forgiveness story. It has all the elements of forgiveness: asking for it, granting it, withholding it, and receiving it. To get the full impact, the story should be read from the point of view of the father, the son, and the elder brother.

Two Men in the Temple
Luke 18:9-14

The parable of the Pharisee and the tax collector has to do with attitudes. "God, be merciful to me, a sinner" is an attitude that is always acceptable to God.

Words From the Cross
Luke 23:32-43

Jesus pronounces a general absolution to all who had anything to do with his crucifixion, "Father, forgive them, for they do not know what they are doing," and then responds to a specific request from one of the thieves on the cross.

The Woman at the Well
John 4:5-30

Jesus speaks to a Samaritan woman—an outcast, according to Jewish tradition—and offers her the gift of "living water."

The Woman Taken in Adultery
John 8:3-11

Jesus intervenes in the execution of a woman discovered in adultery. He does not flatly condemn her, but tells her to "go and sin no more."

Peter and Jesus are Reconciled
John 18:25-27; 21:1-17

Contrast the first passage which records Peter's denial of Jesus before the crucifixion with the post-resurrection encounter between the two men at the Sea of Tiberias. The story is a tender study of reconciliation.

Other Significant Passages

Happy are those whose transgression is forgiven, whose sin is covered (Ps. 32:1).

Create in me a clean heart, O God, and put a new and right spirit within me (Ps. 51:10).

But there is forgiveness with you, so that you may be revered (Ps. 130:4).

Come now, let us argue it out, says the Lord: though your sins are like scarlet, they shall be like snow; though they are red like crimson, they shall become like wool (Is. 1:18).

I have no pleasure in the death of the wicked, but that the wicked turn from their ways and live (Ezek. 33:11).

Come to me, all you that are weary and are carrying heavy burdens, and I will give you rest (Mt. 11:28).

Do not judge, and you will not be judged; do not condemn, and you will not be condemned. Forgive, and you will be forgiven (Lk. 6:37).

Be on your guard! If another disciple sins, you must rebuke the offender, and if there is repentance, you must forgive (Lk. 17:3).

For God so loved the world that he gave his only Son, so that everyone who believes in him may not perish but may have eternal life (John 3:16).

All this is from God, who reconciled us to himself through Christ, and has given us the ministry of reconciliation (2 Cor. 5:18).

In Christ God was reconciling the world to himself (2 Cor. 5:19).

And be kind to one another, tenderhearted, forgiving one another, as God in Christ has forgiven you. Eph (4:32).

The saying is sure and worthy of full acceptance, that Christ Jesus came into the world to save sinners—of whom I am the foremost (1 Tim. 1:15).

The prayer of faith will save the sick, and the Lord will raise them up; and anyone who has committed sins will be forgiven (Jas. 5:15).

But if anyone does sin, we have an advocate with the Father, Jesus Christ the righteous; and he is the atoning sacrifice for our sins, and not for ours only but also for the sins of the whole world (1 John 2:1-2).

Form of Self-Examination

Using the Ten Commandments and Jesus' Summary of the Law

The following form of self-examination is suggested for times of meditation and reflection and as an outline in preparing for a formal confession. I personally like to make notes on a yellow pad as I go along. Nevertheless, it's your self-exam. Use it any way you like.

I have based my outline on the Ten Commandments, which can be found in Exodus 20:1-17 and Deuteronomy 5:6-21. They can also be found in the Book of Common Prayer, pp. 317-318, 350 and 847-848. Roughly they can be divided into duty towards God and duty towards others. I am including Jesus' summary of the law, as it also includes love for one's self.

One of the scribes came near and heard them disputing with one another, and seeing that he answered them well, he asked him, "Which commandment is the first of all?" Jesus answered, 'The first is, 'Hear, O Israel: the Lord our God, the Lord is one; and you shall love the Lord your God with all your heart, and with all your soul, and with all your mind, and with all your strength.' The second is this, 'You shall love your neighbor as yourself.' There is no other commandment greater than these" (Mk. 12:28-31).

In My Relationship with God

1. Do I put God first in my life?

2. Have I ever really made a commitment of all that I am and all that I have to God through Jesus Christ as Lord and Savior?

3. Am I willing to renew the commitment I made at my baptism and confirmation?

4. Do I allow other concerns, anxieties, or fears to get in the way of my trust relationship with God?

5. Have I allowed such things as ambition, career, money, popularity, reputation, power, control, etc., to get in the way of my relationship to God?

6. Do I dabble in or flirt with occult or non-Christian superstitious practices?

7. Do I treat God's name, and the Lord's name, with respect and reverence? Do I use it as a curse? Do I use God's name to manipulate others? Do I use the Lord's name in a self-serving manner?

8. Am I faithful as a member of the Body of Christ? Am I present and do I participate in the worship services in my parish?

9. Do I support the work of my church through my tithe, talent, and time?

10. Am I developing good habits of prayer, Bible reading, and study?

In My Relationship with Others

1. Am I responsible in my relationships to members of my family, treating them with respect and courtesy and allowing them the freedom to be the special creation God made them to be?

2. Do I ever resort to or advocate violence or bodily harm? Do I have habits which put the lives of others in danger (i.e., driving at excessive speeds or skateboarding through a crowded shopping mall)? Do I hold onto hatreds of individuals or groups of people?

3. Am I faithful in my marriage vows? Do I respect the marriage vows of others? Do I allow myself to indulge in pornography or sexual fantasy? Am I willing

to place all of my physical needs and drives under the Lord's dominion and control?

4. Do I respect the space, property, and ideas of others?

5. Am I willing to share my wealth and possessions with those who are less fortunate than I? Am I willing to work for justice and peace among all persons?

6. Do I give an honest day's work for an honest day's pay? When employing or contracting for the service of others, am I willing to pay a fair price or wage and treat employees with dignity and respect?

7. Do I tell the truth? Do I ever withhold part of the truth? Do I keep my promises and honor my commitments? Do I pass on rumors or gossip which might hurt others? Can I be trusted to keep secrets?

8. Do I want things that don't belong to me, cannot belong to me, and for which I am unable or unwilling to work? Do I dislike, resent, or hate people who have more than I do? (This encompasses money, popularity, recognition, power, beauty, success, etc.)

In My Relationship to Myself

1. Do I love and respect the unique and special creation that I am?

2. Do I accept God's unconditional love for me?

3. When I ask for forgiveness, do I believe and act on the certain knowledge that I have been forgiven?

4. Am I honest with myself?

5. Am I fair with myself?

6. Do I set aside time for recreation, exercise, and rest?

7. Do I set aside time for spiritual growth?

8. Do I allow others to set my agenda?

9. Do I respect and take care of my own body?

Forms of Self-Examination

May God in his love enlighten your heart, that you may remember in truth all your sins and his unfailing mercy.

Form of Self-Examination

Using 1 Corinthians 13

Though I speak with the tongues of men and of angels, and have not love, I am become as sounding brass, or a tinkling cymbal. And though I have the gift of prophecy, and understand all mysteries, and all knowledge; and though I have all faith, so that I could remove mountains, and have not love, I am nothing. And though I bestow all my goods to feed the poor, and though I give my body to be burned, and have not charity, it profiteth me nothing.

1. The first question we need to ask ourselves has to do with love. How am I doing as a loving person?

    a. Is my love short-term or long-suffering?

    b. Have I been kind or unkind?

    c. Do I envy other people's possessions or achievements?

    d. Do I keep calling attention to myself?

    e. Do I look down on other people?

    f. Do I have any annoying habits?

    g. Do I insist on having my own way?

    h. Do I lose my temper?

    i. Do I consider ways to get even with those who have hurt me or disappointed me?

    j. Am I pleased when something bad happens to someone else? Do I enjoy gossip especially when it is juicy?

    k. Am I happy when I hear of someone else's success?

Let Us Pray

Lord, help me to love as you have loved; to bear all things; to believe all things; to endure all things. Lord, I know that your love never fails. Help me to love as you have loved. I know that many things we hold dear will pass away, but that your love will endure. Help the faith of this child to grow into the mature and lasting faith of one of your saints. Help my limited faith which is blurred and dim to grow into clear and bright focus. Give me the grace to grow in faith, hope, and love until I see you face to face. In Jesus' name I pray. Amen.

Examination of Relationships

This is a form that developed out of my own experience. It is *a* way to begin. It is not *the* way to begin. I like to make lists; but before I begin, I say a short prayer. Here is one suggestion.

O Lord, I lift up all my relationships to you, from the most intimate to the merely casual. I place them under your dominion and I pray that you will bring to remembrance any brokenness and lead us to the point of reconciliation. In Jesus' name I pray. Amen.

The next step is to make a list of bruised, injured, or broken relationships, using the suggested categories. You may want to go back over the list and rate the damage—say from 1-10: 1 is mild annoyance, 10 is a killing rage.

RELATIONSHIPS

SPOUSE

PARENTS

CHILDREN

SIBLINGS

OTHER RELATIVES

IN-LAWS

EMPLOYER

EMPLOYEES

CO-WORKERS

FRIENDS:

old

former

new

NEIGHBORS

FELLOW CHURCH MEMBERS

SIGNIFICANT OTHERS*

FORMER SPOUSE(S)

FORMER IN-LAWS

SELF

GOD

*I have in mind here people like the checkout counter clerk who just plain rubs me the wrong way.

Now it is time to pray again, using the names you have noted. Here's a suggestion for a useful prayer.

Father, I lift up_____&_____&_____etc.
Help me to want healing and forgiveness in these relationships. If I'm not there yet, help me to get back to that place where I can forgive and be forgiven, and where it is possible to be reconciled to _____or discover the relationship you have in mind for us. In Jesus' name I pray. Amen.

WARNING: There is not any way you can deal with all the broken relationships at one time, so once you have lifted them all up to the Lord, ask him to direct you to the one that is most pressing. Know that the

Lord will be working on all of them once you have surrendered them into his hands.

MORE CAUTION: If the relationship you are working on is rate 6 or above, you may want to seek the help of a Christian friend, a spiritual director, or your pastor or priest.

First, ask the Lord to forgive you for anything you may have done, or failed to do, that hurt the relationship.

Second, ask the Lord to give you some insight or understanding of why the person who hurt you acted that way.

Third, forgive that person very specifically for whatever they did to hurt you. For instance:

Father, I forgive_____for_____and I pray that you will forgive him/her, too. Amen.

Finally, and this is very important, pray very specifically for that person's well-being. For instance:

Lord, I release_____into your keeping. I pray that_____ will_____. In Jesus' name I pray. Amen.

A man prayed for an ex-spouse: *Lord, I forgive Janet for leaving me. I ask your forgiveness, and hers, for any hurt I may have caused her and I release her into your hands and pray that she may be safe from harm and that she may be happy in her new home with her new husband. Amen.*

When you have done this, know that the transaction is complete. Regardless of what you feel, act on the knowledge that you have cut the offending person loose from the power of that hurt or evil. I believe this statement from John 20:23 is valid here: " If you forgive people's sins they are forgiven and if you do not forgive them they are not forgiven."

Forms of Self-Examination

Since its first publication by Cowley in the US and distribution by SPCK in the UK, *The Forgiveness Book* has gone through four re-printings and received enthusiastic reviews in both the religious and secular press. It has found wide use, not only for individual reading, as a text book in religious studies programs and in small group study in congregations as well. It has been followed by the publication of *Grace Happens* and *Coming To Faith*.